MOTHE

GIPSY FORTUNE TELLER

—AND—

DREAM BOOK,

—WITH—

NAPOLEON'S ORACULUM

Embracing full and correct rules of divination concerning dreams and visions, foretelling of future events, their scientific application to Physiognomy, Physiology, Moles, Cards, Dice, Dominoes, Grounds of Coffee and Tea Cups, etc.; together with the application and observance of Charms, Spells and Incantations. It also gives the true interpretation of dreams, and the lucky numbers of the lottery to which they apply.

A. WEHMAN

MOTHER SHIPTON'S

GIPSY FORTUNE TELLER

—AND—

DREAM BOOK

Dreams, and Their Interpretations; and Numbers of the Lottery to which They Apply.

ABSENCE.—To see absent persons in your dreams is a certain sign of their return. 4, 11.

ABUSE.—To dream that you are abused and insulted is a certain sign that some dispute will happen between you and some person with whom you have business; therefore, after such a dream you should be particularly careful of yourself, and be as gentle and mild as possible, that you may not give those with whom you have dealings any advantage over you. 9, 13.

ACORN.—Denotes poverty. 7, 33.

ACQUISITION.—A favorable sign to the dreamer. 2, 19, 46.

ACTIVITY.—If you dream that you are very active, it shows you will have great losses through your own negligence. 10, 11, 75.

ACTRESS.—To see one play, misfortune; if you talk with her, you will have success in what you undertake; if you make love to her, your life will be joyful. If you dream that you enjoy her, you will meet great troubles. 14, 36, 52.

ADOPTION.—To dream of adopting children foreshadows sorrow and trouble. 21.

ADMIRATION.—If you dream that you are admired, it foretells good fortune; but if you admire any one else, it is a very bad sign. 59, 71.

ADULTERY.—If you commit it in your dreams, you must prepare for misfortune and disgrace. 1, 11, 39.

AGUE.—To dream you have an ague denotes nothing very particular more than that you are in danger of becoming a drunkard and a glutton. To dream your sweetheart has an ague is a lucky omen; it shows you are beloved, and that you will be happy with the object of your wishes, but never very rich. 9, 7, 4.

AIR.—If you dream that it is clear, it signifies that you will come into a great fortune; if the air is foggy, you will have sorrows; if it is filled with sweet odors, you will be successful in love. 42.

ALMONDS.—Signify embarrassments, all which you may avoid by care; to eat them, good fortune. 61, 76.

ALTAR.—To dream you see an altar, betokens your speedy marriage. 36, 51, 57, 62.

ANGEL.—To dream of an angel brings joyous tidings; if the angel does not approach you, it is a sign that your life is evil and a warning to reform. 14, 65.

ANTS.—To dream of them shows covetousness. If they are winged, you will make a dangerous voyage, or meet with an accident. The dream is good for farmers, ploughmen, and public servants. 2, 7, 41.

APE.—To see one in your dreams shows that you will fall into the hands of sharpers; and that some enemy will endeavor to defraud you. 4, 5, 6, 31.

APRICOTS.—To see them shows that you will be disappointed in what you hope for; to eat them, good fortune. If it is not the season for them, it denotes great misfortunes; if they are dry, they bring sorrow. 28, 40, 78.

APPAREL.—If you dream that you have new clothes, it denotes prosperity and happiness; if the garments are white, it is a bad dream for all persons except clergymen; to mechanics it signifies loss of business; to the sick, death. If, however, they dream of black, it is a sign of recovery. If they are scarlet, it is a good dream for rich men and servants, but death to the sick and loss to the poor; to dream of woman's apparel is good for the unmarried, but to the married, man, loss of wife and children. 4, 13.

APPARITION.—Of any kind is a very bad sign. 20.

APPLES.—If you take them from the tree, it signifies that you will be persecuted. If they are ripe and ruddy, and you eat them, it will bring much happiness. If they are sour, you will shortly quarrel with some one. 4, 11, 44.

ARM.—To dream that you have the right arm cut off is significant of the death of a female relative; if both arms are cut off, captivity and sickness; an arm broke or withered, sorrows, losses, and widowhood; an arm swollen, sudden fortune falling to a dear friend; to dream that you have strong arms signifies health and happiness;

dirty arms, misery; hairy arms, an increase of fortune and family. 3, 70.

ARMY.—If victorious, good tidings; but if routed, you must prepare for misfortune. 52.

ARCHBISHOP.—To dream of one, you will hear of the death of a friend. 13.

ARTICHOKE.—To see them foretells secret trouble: if you eat them, you may expect to have trouble. 12.

ARTIST.—To dream of artists shows that you will have many pleasures. 27.

ASHES.—Are significant of mourning. 17, 30.

ASS.—If you see him running, brings misfortune; if he is tied fast, you will be slandered; if you hear him bray, you will experience great loss. 44.

AUTHOR.—To see one or more is a bad sign; you will lose money. To dream that you are an author signifies misery and disappointed hope. 1.

AUTOMATON.—Signifies servitude and bondage to him who dreams of them. 19.

BACON.—To dream of bacon denotes the death of some friend or relation, and that enemies will endeavor to do you a mischief; in love it denotes a disappointment of some kind. 21.

BACK.—To see your own back denotes a fortune and premature old age; to dream that your back is broke and full of sores means that your enemies will persecute you and turn you into ridicule. 27, 43.

BACKGAMMON.—To play a game signifies that you will quarrel with a dear friend; if you win, success in love and business; if you lose the reverse. 29, 52.

BAKING.—For a woman to dream she is baking bread foretells thrift. If she is a farmer's wife, it is a sign of good crops. If she burns her bread, it is a sign that she will have a miscarriage. 3, 136.

BALL.—To dream that you are at a ball denotes that money will be left to you. 39, 53, 68.

BALLET.—Joy and boundless pleasure will be your lot. 6.

BALLOON.—To dream of it shows that you will engage in many chimerical plans. 45, 59, 68.

BANDITS.—If you attack them, rely upon your own judgment and vigor; if they attack you, beware of accidents; if you only see them, it denotes prosperity in your business. 1, 13, 20.

BANISHMENT.—You will have sorrow, but of short duration. 59.

BANK.—You will be misled by deceitful promises. 4, 5, 11, 44.

BANKRUPT.—A bad dream; your business is in a dangerous position, and without great care you will be forced to stop. 17, 78.

BANQUET.—To dream that you are at a banquet is a caution to avoid pleasures which may cost you dear. 30, 60.

BARN.—Filled with grain, a rich marriage; you will gain a lawsuit; it also signifies that you will live a happy life. 10, 44.

BARRELS.—Signify wealth if they appear full; if empty, poverty. 14.

BASIN.—If you dream that it is full, money; if empty, you will make many debts. 2, 13.

BATS.—If black, you will quarrel; white, bring pleasure and happiness. 4, 30.

BATH.—To dream that you bathe in clear water, is a sign that you will enjoy good health; if muddy, the death of relatives or friends. To see a bath, anger; to take a warm bath denotes happiness; if you take one either too hot or too cold, domestic troubles. If you undress, without going into the water, you may expect trouble, but it will soon pass away; a sea bath is a sign of honor and increase of fortune. 6, 8, 16.

BATTLE.—If you take part in it, you have much cause to fear disaster; you will have misfortune in love and business; if you finish it, you will have quarrels in your family affairs. 8, 14, 29.

BAYONET.—This is a sign which you should fear. 2, 9, 15.

BEAM.—You will become great, but beware of falling. 1, 8.

BEANS.—Disputes and quarrels. 2, 20, 25.

BEAR.—If you are attacked by it, you will be persecuted by enemies; but if it is running, happiness is in store for you. 44, 64.

BEARD.—If you dream you have a long beard, it signifies that you will live long; if the beard be quite black, great trouble will be your lot; a red beard denotes shame and disgrace to the dreamer; to dream of being shaved betokens loss and disappointment; if you shave yourself, despondency; if somebody pulls your beard, you will have losses; to dream you shave a young girl denotes a good and speedy marriage; if you shave a married lady, she will soon become a widow; if you shave a pregnant woman, she will have a son. 12,40.

BEATING.—For married people to dream of beating some one shows that they will live a peaceful life; to bachelors, good fortune in their amours; if a lover beats his mistress, or a lady her suitor, it shows that the match will be broken off. To beat a dog signifies fidelity; a cat treachery; a snake, you will triumph. 41.

BED.—To dream that you are lying in bed signifies that you are in danger; being in bed and not able to sleep, sickness; to see a stranger in your bed brings quarrels in married life; a well-made bed shows that you will become established in life. 1, 62, 70.

BEDBUGS.—Bring strife. 20.

BEER.—To drink it, trouble. 42, 70.

BEERHOUSE.—To meet your friends there signifies joy and pleasure. 42, 47, 49.

BEES.—They signify wealth and success in business; if they sting you, a friend will betray you; if the dreamer kills a bee, he will have great losses; seeing bees leave their honey is a sign of honor and fortune; if they fly into their hives, losses through enemies. 3, 4, 16, 55.

BEGGAR.—To be a beggar, you may hope for wealth; to see many, sickness. 26.

BELL.—Misfortunes for the person who hears it ring. 6.

BELLY.—To dream one's belly is bigger and fuller than ordinary shows his family and estate will increase; if one dreams his belly is grown lean and shrunk up, he will be joyfully delivered of some bad accident; if any one dreams that his belly is swelled, and yet notwithstanding be empty, he will become poor; if a girl dreams of a big belly, it is a sign of marriage. 14, 6.

BET.—To dream that you bet with any one shows that you will suffer from your own imprudence. 66.

BILL.—If presented to you and you settle it, good luck; if you cannot pay, it signifies that you will be slandered. 4, 11, 44.

BIRDS.—Are a good sign; they bring friends and fortune; to catch them, speedy marriage; to kill them, bad fortune; to shoot at them, beware of treachery; if you see them fighting, you will be exposed to great temptations; if they fly towards you, you will fail in business; if they sing, some happiness is in store for you; to dream of birds of prey, brings misfortune. 2, 11, 19, 22.

BITE.—To dream that you are bitten foretells much jealousy and sorrow. 15, 18.

BLASPHEMY.—If you dream that you are cursing, it foretells bad fortune; if you are cursed, all your expectations will be fulfilled. 25, 58.

BLOOD.—To dream that you see blood is a good sign; you will fall heir to an estate. To lose blood signifies sorrow and disappointment. 5, 10, 40.

BOAR.—Success in life to him who kills one; if he only sees it, danger and misfortune. 4, 44, 76, 77.

BOAT.—Seen in a clear stream, happiness; in muddy water, disgrace; if it is in danger of capsizing, trouble. 17, 12.

BOOKS.—To be reading serious books shows honor and station in life; to read lascivious books, shame and disgrace. 31.

BOOTS.—If they are new, success in love and business; if they are old, quarrelling and failure. 29, 77.

BOTTLES.—To dream of bottles is a good sign; to a man, success in business; to a maid, speedy marriage; if they are broken, they signify sorrow. 4, 6, 10, 24, 50.

BOUQUET.—To receive one, much pleasure; to give one, signifies that your lover is constant. 1, 29, 63.

BOY.—If a lady dreams that she is delivered of a boy, her life will be a pleasant one. 1, 12, 40.

BREAD.—To eat wheaten bread, gives great gain to the rich, but loss to the poor; to eat rye bread is the reverse. 48.

BREAKFAST.—To dream that you are eating breakfast shows that you will commit some folly. 30, 36, 59.

BREAST.—To dream that you have a rough, strong breast shows that you will enjoy good health; a large breast, for man, portends good luck; but for a woman, the loss of her husband. 36, 45.

BRIARS.—To dream that you are among briars and get pricked foretells that you will have an angry dispute with somebody. If a young girl who has a lover dreams it, she will probably get vexed at him. 8, 7.

BRIDGE.—To pass one shows success in life through industry; to fall from one, loss of business and disappointment in love. 2, 13, 19, 24, 56.

BUILDING.—To dream of seeing a large building is a sign that you will be introduced to some one with whom you will afterwards become intimate. To a young lady it predicts that she will have a new admirer. 5, 114.

BULL.—If you dream you were chased by a bull and run away from him, it is a sign that some one will offer you a present, or propose to benefit you in some way, and that you will either decline, or from some action of your own will not receive the present or the benefit. If you do not run away from the bull, but stand your ground and dodge him, you will then have a piece of good luck of some kind.

BURIED ALIVE.—To dream that you are buried alive denotes that you will be rich and powerful. To wealthy people it is a sign of addition to their wealth. 3, 69.

BURNING.—To see in your dream one or more houses burning, but not wholly destroyed, signifies, for the poor, that they will become rich; and for the rich man that his riches will be augmented; but if the fire is furious and the houses fall down, the dreamer may expect losses, disappointments, shame and death. If he sees his bed burning, sickness; to see furniture and clothing, or curtains burning is significant of trouble. A store seen burning, loss of business; to see the front windows of a house burning, death of a brother; rear windows, death of a sister; a burning door, trouble for a housekeeper. To see a man burning in bed foretells loss of goods and sickness; to see one's finger burnt shows that some one is envious of you. To dream that you are burning to death shows that you will soon be engaged in a furious quarrel. 31, 36, 77.

BUSINESS.—To dream of being full of business is significant of some unexpected good fortune; to finish it, marriage; if the business appears to be bad, it is a good sign. 17, 21.

BUTCHER.—If, in your dream, you see a butcher killing any animal, it is a sign of the death of a friend or near relative. If a farmer dreams of seeing sheep killed, he will probably have a prolific flock. 9, 6.

BUTTER.—If you eat it, you will be surprised by some good fortune, but mixed with sadness. 4, 7, 13.

CABBAGE.—Bad tidings. 9, 30.

CAGE.—Without a bird, means imprisonment; with bird, liberty. 11.

CAKES.—To see them made, treachery; to eat them, for women, disappointment, and loss of lovers and property. 19, 38.

CANDLE.—If it burns brightly, happiness; if the light be dim, misfortune; if you light it, success in what you undertake. 21, 66, 78.

CANDY.—To dream that you are eating candy signifies that you will be a victim to falsehood and flattery. 38, 51, 56.

CANNON.—A sign of treachery and danger; to hear one, death. 56.

CANNON-BALL.—To see one, misfortune. 40, 51.

CAMEL.—To see a camel foretells riches. 22.

CAP.—To put one on, be careful in your love affairs; to take one down shows that which you wish to hide will be discovered; if you receive a cap, you will soon be married. 13.

CARRIAGE.—To ride in one, success in love and riches; if it breaks down, you will lose your lover. 57.

CART.—Its appearance indicates sickness; if you go upon it, or move from it, public disgrace and shame. 69.

CAT.—Signifies treachery of friends and disappointment in affairs of love; if the cat appears to be lying down or sleeping, you will but partially succeed in what you may undertake; if the cat is fighting, or appears to be in a rage, you will be robbed. 14.

CATERPILLAR.—You will be slandered by envious persons. 10, 20, 34, 40.

CAVERN.—A deep cavern shows that you will always remain poor and unknown, unless you exert yourself. 46, 51.

CELLAR.—Signifies sickness and misery. 12, 27, 36.

CHAINS.—To wear them melancholy; to break them, gives future happiness. 41, 56.

CHARITY.—For a rich person to dream that he is charitable signifies loss of fortune; if a lady dreams it, she will bestow her affections on an unworthy person. 1, 16, 56.

CHEESE.—Anger; to eat it, gain. 5, 15, 66.

CHESS.—If you play chess with any one, you will quarrel with your dearest friend; to win a game shows success in a difficult undertaking; losing it, you will be foiled. 17.

CHESTNUTS.—To eat them raw shows resolution; boiled, weakness. 44, 78.

CHICKEN.—Its cooking is the sign of coming good news. 2.

CHILD.—To see a child at its mother's breast signifies severe sickness; but if the wife of the dreamer be pregnant, the child will be sickly. To see many children, and to talk with them, shows great losses for the dreamer. 1, 19, 67, 69.

CHIMNEY.—To dream of sitting in the chimney-corner, to a maid, shows speedy marriage; if there is a fire burning brightly, you will become heir to some money. 5, 66.

CHOCOLATE.—To drink it foretells good health and a happy life. 10.

CHRISTENING.—To dream that you are present at a christening is a good sign you will get what you hope for; to a maid it signifies that she will soon be married. 4, 25, 26.

CHURCH.—To dream of building a church is a good sign to the dreamer; to enter one, you will receive a kindness from some one; to play in one, success and marriage. 2, 19, 33.

CHURCHYARD.—Makes a happy life. 36, 60.

CIGAR.—To the man who smokes it, success; if it be not lit, it signifies misfortune; if he light it, he may hope. 1, 8, 20.

CITY.—To dream of an inhabited city is a sign of riches; a burning city, poverty. 4.

CLIMBING.—If you climb a tree, you will rise to honor. 16.

CLOTHING.—Clothed in rags signifies mourning and trouble; to wear good clothes, a happy life; dirty clothes, disgrace; to steal clothing, gives success in love and business. To wear clothing of many colors foretells disappointed hopes. 21, 69.

CLOUDS.—Signify disunion; light clouds, happiness; black clouds, misfortune. 39, 76.

COACH.—If you dream you are riding in a coach, it signifies loss of reputation. For a young girl to have such a dream predicts the loss of her virtue. 14, 8, 6.

COALS.—Burning, persecution; if put out by water, death. 18, 45.

COCK.—To hear a cock crow in sleep, is a good sign; it brings good news. 22, 43. To dream you see a cock in the house, is a good sign to those who would marry; to hear a cock crow denotes great prosperity. 6, 5, 4.

COFFEE.—A sign of misfortune. 11,12, 39.

COFFIN.—To dream of a coffin signifies that you will soon be married and own a house of your own. 9, 49, 50.

COLLAR.—A good dream; it brings honor. 55, 65, 78.

COMEDY.—To dream that you act in a comedy, you should prepare to hear bad news; if you see it played, you will succeed in your undertaking. 15.

CONCERT.—To dream of being at a concert foretells the enjoyment of good health; to the sick, recovery. 12, 27.

CONFECTIONERY.—Profitable to the dreamer. 19, 20.

CORN.—To see it blooming shows an increase of your family. 41, 46.

CORPSE.—A good sign, you will soon be married. 9, 77.

CRABS.—Signify quarrels and separation. 3, 30.

CRADLE.—A child's cradle, many children; if the cradle be of green leaves, loss and sorrow. 1.

CRAZY.—If a person dreams that he is crazy, he will receive presents, and become rich, and live many years. 33, 43, 63.

CRIMINAL.—To dream that you are a criminal shows that disgrace and danger are in store for you. 9, 10, 61.

CROSS.—To dream of a cross brings success and honor. To carry it, trouble. 10, 40.

CROWN.—To dream a golden crown is placed upon your head foretells that success and great honor await you; if the crown be silver, you will enjoy good health; if crowned with green leaves, friends and fortune will forsake you. 42, 52, 67.

CRUTCHES.—If you use them, your love will forsake you; if you only see them, some infirmity will press upon you; if you break them, you will recover from sickness. 55, 77.

CURRANTS.—To dream of eating white currants, brings some happy tidings; red currants, show that your lover is constant; black ones, marriage. 1, 2, 10.

CYPRESS.—Signifies misfortune. 37.

DAGGER.—To dream of a dagger, you may expect news of absent persons. 63.

DANCE.—To be at a dance, shows success in love and friendship. 11, 17, 55.

DANGER.—To dream of being in danger shows success in life; to shun it, misfortune. 18.

DAY.—To dream of a clear day, is a happy sign. 3, 24, 60.

DEEDS.—To sign your name to deeds is a bad sign; to a man, loss in business; to a woman, the inconstancy of her lover. 71.

DEER.—If you see it, you will receive good news; if you kill it, you will fall heir to an estate. 4, 8, 60.

DEVIL.—Superstitious people may dream of seeing this arch-enemy of mankind. If so, it foretells that they will go away from home to be absent some time. It also shows that they will be very fortunate in life. To a young girl it is a sign that she will either be well married and leave home, or leave for some other reason. 6, 9.

DICE.—To dream of playing with dice is a sign of disgrace, or that you will do some act that, if it is not bad in itself, will cause people to censure you for. To a young girl engaged to be married, dreaming of dice foretells that her lover will be wild and not of much account. 8, 7.

DIFFICULTY.—If you imagine in your dream that you are in great difficulty, or in personal danger of any kind, it is a favorable sign, as such dreams always go by contrary. If you fear you are about losing money, you will get some; if your life is in peril, it foretells happiness; if you imagine your sweetheart snubs you, she'll surely be kind and willing, etc. 5, 6, 9.

DIGGING.—To dream of digging in clean and healthy ground is a sign of thrift and good luck generally; if the ground be dirty or wet, it shows trouble; if you are digging for gold and find large and rich lumps, it shows you'll have some good luck, but if the product is meagre, or if you don't find any, it foretells disappointment. If you lose any of your tools, it is a sign of a quarrel. 65, 8.

DINNER.—If you dream of sitting down to dinner with a large company, it is a sign you will either go a journey or change the present location either of your dwelling or business. 31.

DIRT.—To roll in the dirt, poverty; to have dirt thrown at you, sickness and slander. 11, 33, 64. To dream of dirty dirt or mud signifies that some one will speak ill of you. If it is clean sand or soil, and you do not get befouled with it, it is a sign of thrift and good fortune. If some one throws dirt on you, it foretells that you will be abused. 62, 78.

DISEASE.—If you dream you have any contagious or foul disease on you, it foretells luck and benefit, as such a dream goes by contrary. If you dream of a running sore, it shows that you will have plenty of money and spend it freely. If a young girl dreams she has any contagious disease, she will probably fall in love soon after. 19, 68.

DISPUTE.—A bad sign, if you are in the wrong. 65.

DITCHES.—To dream of ditches, steep mountains, rocks, and other eminences foretells danger and misfortune; expect thieves to rob your dwelling, or that your children will be undutiful, and bring you into trouble; if you are in love, it foretells unhappiness if you marry your present sweetheart. 3, 21, 26.

DOG.—To dream of a dog shows that your friends are faithful; if he appears to be sleeping, you need have no fears; but if he runs and barks, pay attention to yourself and your affairs; if he runs behind you, somebody is slandering you; if he is fighting with another dog, fear persecution; if with a cat, you will quarrel; coupled with a slut, you will be guilty of dissipation and vice. 4, 50.

DOVES.—Significant of good in games of chance: success in amours and pleasures. 1, 22, 29.

DROWNING.—For a man to dream of drowning brings happiness to him; for a female, a lover and happy marriage. 32, 60.

DRUNKENNESS.—To dream of being drunk portends riches and health; if a person dreams that he is drunk, without having tasted liquor, it is a very bad sign: he will shortly commit some bad action; to become drunk with good wine means that he will make the acquaintance of a person of high station. To be drunk and feel sad indicates treachery of relatives. To be drunk and vomit signifies loss of fortune by gambling. If a person dreams of being intoxicated by drinking water, it shows that he will boast untruly of having rich and grand connections. To see a drunken man shows that you will be guilty of some foolish action. 13, 18, 42.

DUEL.—To be present at a duel brings quarrels and rivalry in love; to fight a duel denotes anger; to be wounded, sorrow; to dream that you are killed signifies the divorce of your wife and the loss of a friend. To kill another person, the death of a friend. 5, 16.

DUET.—With a lady, court her and you will win her; with a man, beware of him. 10, 16.

DUNG.—To dream of it denotes that you will be brought to shame and misery by dissipation. 20, 25, 31, 60.

EAGLES.—To see one in your sleep, flying above you, is a good sign; if it lights upon your head, some accident will befall you; if it convey you into the air, some relative or friend will die. 2, 8, 40.

EARTHQUAKE.—To dream of, foretells sickness. 14, 17, 20.

EATING.—To dream of eating, shows that you are deceived; to eat broiled meat, good fortune; to eat turnips, quarrelling; to eat salad, sickness. 2, 21, 69.

ECLIPSE.—Of the sun, foretells great losses; of the moon, small misfortunes. 14, 56.

EEL.—To dream of catching a live eel signifies that you are in danger from the malice and treachery of enemies. If dead, misfortune. 7, 17.

EGGS.—Mean happiness; to see many broken eggs is a sign of quarrelling and lawsuits; fresh eggs, good news. 8, 39, 65, 66.

ELEPHANT.—To see one, fear and danger for the rich; to give him food, some great person will befriend you; to get on his back, good fortune. 62, 78.

ELOPEMENT.—Signifies an offer of marriage. 18, 25, 66.

ENTERPRISE.—If you dream that you are engaged in some great enterprise, it shows that you will miscarry in what you have already undertaken. 1, 24.

ENTRAILS.—To see them is a good sign, if they belong to another person; but if to yourself, it is bad. 14, 19.

EMBRACE.—To dream of embracing relatives is a warning of treachery; if friends, disappointments; if one unknown embrace you, you will travel; the embrace of a woman brings good luck. 19, 69.

EMBROIDERY.—To dream of embroidery shows that you are proud and ambitious; to wear an embroidered dress signifies honor and wealth. 1, 16, 79.

ERUPTIONS.—To dream of your body being covered with blotches shows that a great fortune will fall to you. 12, 24.

EVENING.—To dream of it, danger. 6, 12, 60.

EXCUSE.—To seem to be making excuses in your dreams shows that you will tell lies. 71, 75.

EYE.—If you dream you see a person with a defective eye, it denotes disappointment; to see a glaring squint-eye in your dream shows that you will be defeated or crossed in some enterprise. To dream that your own eyes are defective, or squint, is a sure sign of bad luck; sore eyes denote sickness; blindness, death. 3, 8, 6.

EYES.—If you appear to be handsome, shows happiness; dull eyes indicate faults over which you will have much grief; loving eyes, your mistress will be unfaithful to you; eyes shut, your wife is jealous of you, with reason. If a person dreams that he has lost his eyesight, he will lose a dear friend. 6, 66, 72.

FACE.—To dream your face is swelled shows that you will accumulate wealth; if you are in love, it denotes that your sweetheart will receive an unexpected legacy and marry you. To see a handsome woman's face means joy and pleasure; if a woman sees a handsome man, she will shortly be married to the one she desires. 7, 8.

FAINTING.—To dream of fainting shows you are wanton. 3, 11, 29.

FAIRY.—If you dream of seeing a fairy, you will meet a woman who will seduce you from the path of propriety and make your life vexatious. 1, 7, 16.

FALLING.—If you dream that you fall down, but rise again quickly, you will attain too much honor; but if, on the contrary, you remain where you fell, you will live obscure and in poverty. 21, 30, 37.

FAREWELL.—To say farewell, or to hear another say it, is a bad sign; you will hear painful news. 5, 40.

FAT.—To eat fat, you will overcome all obstacles; to cut it, loss of fortune and friends. 3, 14, 17.

FATIGUE.—To dream of being very tired foretells that you will be well rewarded for your industry. 29, 39, 71.

FAN.—Your mistress will be inconstant. 5, 23, 31.

FAULT.—If you dream you commit a fault, be very careful in your conduct; if you see a fault in a lady who is very dear to you, should you trust her, she will be faithful to you in everything. 18, 78.

FAVOR.—To dream you ask a favor of a person of high standing means loss of time in seeking that which you cannot obtain. To win the favors of a woman signifies that the lady you love bestows her regard on another and laughs at you. 49.

FEAR.—To feel fear signifies that you will be courageous in your waking moments; to dream of frightening others shows that your courage is weak. 19, 46, 62.

FEET.—To dream that your feet are cut off foretells pain; washing them signifies gluttony; lame and dirty feet, sickness; to dream of having many feet shows that one of yours is in danger. This dream for a merchant is a very good omen. To burn a foot is a bad sign. If your feet appear to be light, and you seem to be dancing, you will have much pleasure and many friends. To kiss another person's feet shows abasement and disgrace. Sore feet means losses in journeys, delays and hindrances in business; limping feet foretells shame. If the dreamer is in prison, he will be found guilty and punished; if he is rich, he will lose part of his property by fire. 1, 5, 10, 20, 40.

FIDDLE.—If you hear it played, it brings happiness in your domestic life; if it be silent, mourning; if you play upon it, you will engage in desperate enterprises. 11, 60.

FIELD.—Persecution; to be in a field, deception through false and unworthy friends. 11, 16, 72.

FIGHT.—To see women fighting, signifies jealousy; men, sorrow. 4, 9, 48, 57.

FIGS.—To dream of eating good figs signifies joy and happiness; if the figs are mouldy or defective, your pleasure will be marred by some disagreeable event. Engaged lovers who dream of this fruit will probably experience some fortunate surprise at their wedding if it comes off soon after the dream. To eat them signifies future fortune; if they are out of season, many sorrows; if they are dry, your happiness is at stake. 6.

FIGURES.—All figures below 78 signify success; above 78, uncertainty. 20, 42.

FINE.—To dream you pay a fine signifies gain. 1.

FINGER.—A scalded finger signifies envy; a cut finger, grief; to see more fingers than five shows new relatives. 5, 11, 55.

FIRE.—If it is blazing furiously, danger and separation of friends; if it is extinguished, poverty. If a female makes a fire without much trouble, she will have fine healthy children; if she has much difficulty in kindling it, she will meet with shame and dishonor. If you burn yourself, you will have a fever. A sparkling fire denotes money in abundance. 6, 46, 69.

FLAG.—If you see it waving, it signifies danger; if you bear it, honor and glory. 21, 40.

FLESH.—If a person dream that he is becoming fleshy, he will soon be rich and spend much money on dress. If you dream you are wasting away, you will soon become poor. To imagine your flesh sunburnt, denotes, to a man, treacherous friends; to a woman, adultery and divorce. To see one's flesh yellow is a prediction of wasting fever. To see your flesh full of scars and bugs signifies great riches. To dream that you eat the flesh of another man bids you beware of acquiring property by foul means. 13, 14, 29.

FLOUR.—Death in your neighborhood. 21, 56, 72.

FLOWERS.—To see them in season and of bright colors signifies a pleasant and amorous life; to see them out of season and white, the frustration of your plans; if they appear yellow, bad success in your undertakings. Red flowers denote courage. To receive flowers, success in love. 42, 50.

FOOL.—To dream you are a fool foretells happiness and friends and the birth of children. 19, 20, 30, 54, 60.

FOREHEAD.—To dream that you see yourself having a handsome forehead shows that you possess great spirit; if it is very much rounded, it is a sign of good fortune. To dream that you have a forehead of iron, steel, or brass shows that you carry extreme hatred to your enemies. A large, fleshy forehead shows eloquence, courage, and power. 46, 57.

FORK.—Beware of flattery. 17, 23.

FOUNTAIN.—To dream you are at a fountain of clear water is a very favorable omen to every one; it denotes lucrative operations in business matters, and great happiness and success in love and marriage. If the waters are muddy or roiled, it foretells that your good luck will be attended with troubles and vexations. To see a fountain of clear water signifies joy with profit; if the water be dirty, loss and disappointment; if you have much trouble to get at the water, it shows that you will change your place of residence. A dry fountain signifies poverty and wretchedness. 55, 62.

FOX.—A sign of thieves; to dream of fighting with them, shows that you will have to deal with some cunning enemy; to keep a tame fox signifies that you will love a lewd woman, or have a bad servant, who will rob you. A number of foxes, false friends. 4, 7, 11.

FRIENDS.—To dream of being among friends, to young persons, signifies union; to laugh with them, quarrels. 5, 27, 56.

FROG.—A frog is a sign of immodesty; frogs, flatterers. 4.

FUNERAL.—To dream of attending a funeral shows that you will probably be soon at a wedding or some gay party. If, in your dream, you see a funeral pass, it denotes a pleasure party out of doors, such as a picnic or excursion. If a person dream that he is buried alive, he will meet with much misery; if he follows a funeral, it is a sign that he will be present at some grand entertainment or marriage. 3, 5, 11, 29.

GAG.—If you dream that your mouth is stopped by a gag, it denotes that you will soon thereafter be kissed by a pretty girl. To a young girl, such a dream predicts that she will see some gentleman who takes her fancy, and perhaps will fall in love with him. 9, 6.

GAIN.—If acquired justly, you may hope for wealth; if by injustice, you will lose your fortune. 30, 31.

GALLANTRY.—If a man dream that he is very gallant, he will enjoy good health; to a female the same dream brings good luck; to a girl, inconstancy. 27.

GALLOP.—On a bay horse, trouble, which will soon pass away; on a black horse, misfortune; a white horse signifies a life of pleasure. 51.

GALLOWS.—To dream of a gallows is a good omen, as it denotes that you will have a chance to make money, and if you are smart enough to avail yourself of the opportunity, it will be all right. To those embarking in new enterprises such a dream foretells success. To be condemned to the gallows signifies high office to the dreamer; to the lover, marriage to the person desired. 40, 8, 6.

GAMBLING.—To win at gambling shows the death of a friend; to lose, you will change your residence. 2, 22, 56, 77.

GARDEN.—Your fortune will be enlarged. To walk in one, joy. 15, 73.

GARLIC.—To dream of eating garlic is a prediction of quarrels and the discovery of secrets. 49, 56.

GARTER.—Signifies weakness 1.

GIANT.—To dream of being a giant brings danger to the dreamer. To meet one, honor; a happy life to him who overthrows one. 63, 71, 75.

GIFT.—To dream of receiving gifts denotes good luck; you will marry the girl of your choice, and prosper in what you undertake. 42.

GILT.—To have garments covered with gold lace signifies great honor. 49, 60.

GIRDLE.—To wear a girdle denotes economy; to lay it down, wantonness. 3.

GLASS.—To dream of receiving a glass of water signifies that you will soon be married; if you break it, your lover will forsake you. 28, 42, 52.

GLOVES.—To dream of wearing good gloves brings happiness; if the gloves are torn, many disappointments. 4, 24, 57.

GOAT.—A white goat foretells unexpected gain; a black one, misfortune. 17, 27.

GOLD.—The sign of ambition and avarice. 63, 74.

GOOSE.—To see a goose or geese, shows that you will be troubled with disagreeable visitors. 38, 48, 56.

GRAIN.—To see a large field of grain, signifies a good marriage, and good business; to carry grain, weakness. 14, 27.

GRAPES.—A sign of pleasure. To eat white grapes, great gain; black ones, loss. 11, 18, 32, 33.

GRASS.—Poverty. 11.

GRASSHOPPERS.—An unfavorable sign for the sick. 12.

GRAVE.—To dream of seeing one signifies disappointment and sorrow; to a lover, loss of his mistress; to a maid, her sweetheart will forsake her. To come out of a grave denotes success in what is undertaken; if you are in love, you will marry your sweetheart. 19, 51.

GUITAR.—Luck in love affairs, if the dreamer sings and plays on the instrument at the same time. 4, 20, 45.

GUN.—To dream of firing a gun, or hearing the report of a gun, denotes strife; if you imagine some friend fires it, it shows that there will be a difficulty with him. If you dream of killing a bird, squirrel, or other animal by shooting it, it foretells that you will act rashly in some quarrel. For a lover to dream of firing a gun is a sign he will have trouble with his sweetheart. 7, 16. To dream of seeing guns or cam tired shows that you will meet much trouble and fail in what you undertake, If you love, your sweetheart will forsake you. To dream you are being fired at denotes that many dangers will befall you. 7, 18.

HAIL.—Losses, disappointments, and troubles through life. 14, 56, 60.

HAIR.—Black hair, cut short, signifies misfortune; hair glossy, new friends; brown hair, solicitude and despondency. If your hair falls out, loss of a friend; if it is matted, you will have either a long lawsuit or ill success in what you undertake. If your hair appears to be white, be prudent with what money you may have, or you will have great difficulty in gaining more. To a woman the dream of being bald denotes sudden poverty; to a man, much happiness. 1, 16, 40.

HAIR-DRESSING.—Is a sign of danger. If a woman dreams she is dressing the hair of a lady, it brings bad luck to herself; if her hair be dressed by another person, she will marry and become rich. 5, 30.

HAND.—To dream of having white, handsome hands augurs good success in business, and the affection of relatives. To burn your hand or have it cut off signifies to a man loss of his best friends; to a woman, the loss of her husband or a near relative. If a person dream that his hand is becoming smaller, it shows he is in danger from some one of his family. To dream of working with the right brings happiness; with the left, sorrow and misfortune. A hairy hand signifies imprisonment. Clean, ruddy hands denote, for the poor, friends who will assist; to the rich, an idle and dissolute life. To have many hands, luck and high standing: but for thieves this dream predicts that they will be overtaken and punished. To take up fire in the hand, without being burned, means that you will execute all your plans without hindrance. To beat with the hand signifies that the dreamer, if married, will enjoy domestic quiet; if unmarried, that you will regain the love of your sweetheart. For a woman to beat her husband shows that she must be careful how she treats him, although he loves her. If a woman beat her lover, it shows she will lose him. To look at one's own hand, weakness. 5, 16, 45.

HANGED.—To dream that you see a person hanged, or that you are hung yourself, denotes that you will rise to great honor, and that you will better your fortune by marriage. 5, 19.

HARLEQUIN.—Your sweetheart will betray you. 49, 63.

HARP.—To hear a harp played signifies recovery to the sick. 2, 50.

HARE.—To see a hare denotes that the dreamer will engage in some profitable enterprise. 65.

HARVEST.—Significant of success in business. 19, 31.

HATE.—If you feel hatred to a person in a dream, it shows that you are hated by him. 11, 13.

HAT.—If it is torn, shows that the dreamer's life is vicious. 8, 22.

HAY.—Accidents of a dangerous kind. 1, 11, 17.

HEAD.—To dream of having your head prettily dressed shows that you are in danger. 40, 42, 61.

HEART.—Suffering; dangerous sickness; for a married man, a bad dream. 62.

HEAT.—If you dream of being in a place that is extremely hot, or if the weather is so hot that the heat affects you, it shows that some person is preparing either to attack you or give you a good scolding; if you perspire freely, it is a sign you will meet them at advantage, but if you are feverish, it shows that you will be either injured, or else will have your feelings badly hurt. 3, 8, 7.

HEAVEN.—If any one dreams of this abode of the blessed, that he or she is ascending to heaven, or is already enjoying its delights, it shows that some joyful event is to happen, such as the birth of an heir to childless people, good fortune to those who are poor, distinction to the wealthy, and high honors to the ambitious. If lovers have such a dream, it foretells an early marriage under the most auspicious circumstances, and that their wedding will be attended with troops of congratulating friends, who will shower presents upon them. 11, 4.

HELL.—To dream of seeing hell denotes that the dreamer's life is a bad one, and an intimation to him of reformation. 1, 57, 61, 78.

HENS.—To dream of seeing hens that appear happy and are singing is an excellent omen, as it foretells thrift and a large number of children, and domestic enjoyment generally; if the hens are disturbed and cackling, it shows that something will occur to mar your happiness. If you dream of a hen with many young chickens around her, it is a sign that some one in the family will soon get married. If a young girl dreams this, she will possibly get married before the chickens have time to grow up to henhood. 13, 8.

HIDE, OR HIDDEN.—To dream of concealing anything by hiding it, or putting it in an out-of-the-way place, is a sign that some one will reveal a secret that you have told, or will tell of something that you desired to have concealed; if you find anything that was hidden, and expose it to view, it shows that you will be astonished at some piece of scandal or other information that will be told to you in confidence about another person. It is a bad omen for lovers to dream of hiding things, as it predicts that their intimacy will be talked about as suspicious. 6, 9.

HILLS.—To dream of travelling over steep hills shows that you will experience much care and trouble, and meet with many disappointments; to the lover it denotes rivalry. 9, 36.

HIPS.—Stdrong hips signify healthy and handsome children. 6, 8, 45, 55.

HORNS.—To see horns on the head of another person, danger to the dreamer; on your own, wealth and importance. 71, 76.

HONEY.—Pleasure and a happy life. 13.

HORSE.—To see horses in your dreams is symptomatic of good. If a woman dreams that she is mounted on a strong, handsome horse, it shows that she will marry a rich person, who will love her. To fall from a horse denotes misfortune and disappointment. 4, 21, 32, 44.

HOSPITAL.—To dream of being in one, misery. 21.

HOTEL.—To see one denotes a peaceful life and prosperity; to live in one, a mixed existence of pleasure and pain. 45.

HOUSE.—To see a house, you may hope for a fortunate change in your affairs; to dream of possessing one bids you expect misfortune and sickness. 1, 8, 16, 17.

HUNGRY.—To be very hungry in your dreams denotes that you will become rich and honored through your genius and industry. To eat and be satisfied shows a speedy marriage. 10, 12,16, 66.

HUNTING.—To dream of going a-hunting brings an accusation of dishonesty; if you are returning from the chase, good fortune awaits you. 14, 37, 61.

ICE.—It is a very favorable omen to dream of ice; your sweetheart will be of a very amiable temper and faithful. It denotes success and riches to the trader; to the farmer, plentiful harvests. To be sliding or skating on the ice shows that you will engage in some unprofitable undertaking and fail of success. If you love, your sweetheart is fickle and deceives you, and you will not have your desire; to military men, it foretells much trouble. 11, 15, 54.

ILLUMINATION.—To dream of an illumination augurs success in life, and much happiness; if the light begins to disappear, sorrow and many tears will be your portion. 13, 56.

INK.—Denotes that your expectations will be realized. 14, 24, 36, 65.

INN.—To dream of being at an inn, is very unfavorable; it denotes poverty and unsuccessfulness in business; to the lover, the unfaithfulness of his sweetheart; to the tradesman, loss of business and dishonest agents. 5, 28, 47.

INQUEST.—To dream that you are present at a coroner's inquest is a bad sign; you will soon squander your fortune. 47.

INUNDATION.—Misfortunes and troubles. 22, 25.

IRON.—Unfavorable dream; red iron signifies the shedding of blood. 14, 37, 60.

ISLAND.—To dream that you are on a deserted island shows that you will commit some act to disgust your friends and make them cut your acquaintance; be careful how you behave after dreaming such a dream. 8, 11.

ITCH.—To dream you have the itch, or that your body itches, shows that you will shortly receive money. 38, 49.

IVORY.—Denotes to the dreamer that his love is placed on a young and beautiful girl. 53, 55.

IVY.—To dream of seeing this vine running over and covering any house is a sign of poverty, particularly if the ivy grows thick and abundant; if you dream that it covers your own house, the sign is still more sure; for a farmer to dream that he sees ivy covering a tree denotes bad crops. A girl who dreams of being in a bower covered with ivy will probably marry a poor and shiftless man. It also signifies friendship and worthy confidants. 7, 30, 53.

JAIL.—If a man dreams he is confined in a prison or jail, it shows that he will have honors or dignities conferred upon him, as such dreams go contrariwise; if his arrest and imprisonment worries him, it only shows that he will be the more delighted with his new dignities. This is an excellent dream for politicians and office-holders, and as many of that class of people are great rascals, the jail is what they would naturally dream of. 47, 6.

JAR.—To dream that a house is jarred or shaken by an earthquake, an explosion, or anything that may occur outside, is a sign that the head of the family in that house will be sick. Jars of preserved fruit or jellies, seen in a dream, are good omens; if you dream you are presented with one or more of them, it shows that you will be long-lived and thrifty. 7, 34, 18.

JELLY.—To dream of having pots of jelly given to you, or that you are eating jelly, and that plenty of it is around, is a sure sign of long life and good fortune generally; as many pots as are given to you, or as you may have, so many generations will you live to see. The same rule applies to preserved fruits. 6, 9, 11.

JEW.—If you dream that a genuine Israelite comes along and annoys you in any way, it is a sign you will quarrel with your father; if you imagine that he cheats you in a bargain, it predicts that you will probably receive a present from some near relative; on the contrary, if he gives you an advantage in the bargain, it shows that your father, or some elderly relative, will ask a favor of you. 19, 64.

JIG.—To dream of dancing a jig with a lady is a sign she is in love with you, or is pleased with you; and if you like her, you may go in at once for her favor with much confidence. The omen is the same to a girl who dreams. 5, 41.

JEALOUSY.—To be jealous shows that you are betrayed. 70.

JEWELS.—To dream of possessing jewels shows that you will lose something you highly value. If you see jewels, and are tempted to take them, you are in danger of committing some disgraceful action. 23, 46, 60.

JOY.—To be joyful in sleep, is a forerunner of bad tidings. 14.

JUMPING.—To dream of jumping up foretells high station; to jump down, poverty, if you fall; if you alight on your feet you will be neither poor nor rich. To jump in the mire, disgrace. 42, 54.

KEY.—To lose it, signifies hate and anger; to find a key, brings fortune and love. 18, 49, 57, 70.

KING.—To see a king, or speak to one, shows riches and honor. 32.

KISS.—To kiss the earth shows sorrow and care; to kiss the hands of a lady, good luck; if you kiss her face, you will be successful in love and trade, through courage. To be kissed signifies disagreeable visitors. 13, 47.

KNEE.—Broken, poverty; bent knees signify sickness. To dream of falling on the knees denotes misfortune in business. To see a woman's knees, good luck and marriage to the girl of your choice. For a woman to see a man's knee, shows that she will have many male children. 15, 28.

KNIFE.—To dream of knives foretells disputes and anger; to cut any one with a knife shows disappointment in love; to be sharpening a knife signifies success in life. 7, 34, 47.

KNIGHT.—To see an armed knight foretells good fortune; if you put on his armor, be prudent, you are in danger; if you take it off, the danger will pass away. To see the armor, only, you will overcome all difficulties. 7, 30.

LADIES.—To see one, a sign of weakness; many ladies, brings calumny and slander. To see a light-haired one, is a happy event to the dreamer; a brunette, sickness; a pregnant lady, brings good news; a naked lady signifies the death of a relative. To hear a lady speak, without seeing her, foretells departure. 5, 19, 41.

LADDER.—To dream of going up a ladder foretells the possession of wealth; to come down, poverty. 11, 21, 43.

LAND.—To dream of land signifies that you will travel; to live in the country means loss of property. 65.

LAMP.—To light one signifies suffering and sorrow; if it be soon extinguished, you will die young. 56.

LARK.—To dream of the lark shows speedy increase of fortune. 5, 27, 49.

LAUGHTER.—Is a sign of tears. 17, 19, 26, 47.

LAUREL.—Signifies success to men; to women, the birth of children; to girls, speedy marriage. 76.

LAWYER.—To dream of meeting a lawyer brings bad tidings; if you speak to him, you will lose some property; if you hear some one speaking in his favor, you will meet with some misfortune. 15, 34.

LAW.—To dream of instituting a suit at law, or entering a criminal complaint against any one, shows that some enemy will injure you pecuniarily, or that you will lose money by speculation or trade; if you dream you are sued, or prosecuted criminally, the sign is the reverse; you will probably receive money unexpectedly, or be uncommonly successful in your pursuits. 1, 16, 25.

LAWSUIT.—To dream of being engaged in a lawsuit signifies the acquisition of solid friendship. 1, 16, 23, 25.

LAZY.—To dream that you see lazy people lounging around, and that you are"vexed with them, is a sign of bad luck to some of your relatives, who will depend upon you to assist them; if, in your dream, you imagine yourself to be lazy and sleepy over your work, it foretells either sickness or that you will meet with a loss. 7, 8, 56.

LEAN.—To dream of lean and bony cattle, or hogs, is a bad omen, as it foretells short crops to farmers and dull business to other callings; but if you dream that you yourself have grown lean and cadaverous, it shadows forth the best kind of luck and success; it is also an excellent dream to see thin and lean people around. A girl who dreams that her lover has grown lean may be sure he will grow rich in proportion. 4, 9, 6.

LEAVES.—A bad sign. 39, 62, 73.

LEGS.—To see well-shaped legs, health and happiness, losses and had fortune; thin, spindle-shank legs are excellent ones to dream about, as they denote a successful race with fortune. It is not to be supposed that a lover will ever dream of his sweetheart's legs, but if he should do so, he will probably imagine them to be round, plump, and of an alabaster whiteness. 10, 42.

LEOPARDS.—Signify fortune of different kinds; happiness and misfortune following each other in succession. 1, 4, 45.

LETTERS.—To write or receive them, good news. 55.

LETTER-CARRIER.—News of an absent friend. 18, 51.

LIBERTY.—To dream of taking liberties with any one, bids you be careful of them; if others take liberties with you, it shows they intend to cheat you. 10, 27, 30, 50.

LICE.—Signify wealth; abundance of gold and silver. 23, 41, 54.

LIEUTENANT.—Poverty, with honor. 15, 59.

LIGHT.—A burning light signifies recovery to the sick; fortune and honor to the healthy. 31, 53.

LIGHTNING.—If the dreamer sees lightning strike his house, or fall upon his head, it is the sign of the death of a relative. 39, 62, 73.

LILY.—To dream of seeing lilies in season is a good sign; out of season, your hopes will be vain. 1, 6, 14, 27.

LIMP.—To limp, shame. 18, 62.

LION.—To see one denotes admittance to the society of distinguished persons. To fight with a lion signifies a quarrel with a dangerous person. If you overthrow him, victory over trials and sorrows. To sit or ride on the back of a lion denotes the protection of some powerful personage. To dream of eating the flesh of a lion shows some high office in store for you; the skin of a lion augurs great wealth. To see a lion run away predicts great folly. To see a lioness brings good luck to your family. 4, 44, 54, 60.

LIVER.—Appearing to be diseased, dried, or burned, your life and fortune are in danger. To eat the liver of an enemy shows that you will be victorious. 17, 61.

LIZARD.—Misfortune through false and deceitful friends. 12, 40.

LOOKING-GLASS.—The sign of treachery. 3, 21, 26.

LOVE.—To dream that you are enslaved by the love of a woman shows a sorrowful life; not to return the love of a woman, success; to love a young girl, joy; a handsome woman, wantonness; to love an old woman, misery. 13, 47.

MALLOW.—Deliverance from sorrow, and good business. 19.

MANAGER.—To dream you are manager of any concern, means poverty; if you forsake it, your affairs will immediately improve. 8.

MARBLE.—37, 39.

MAN.—Dressed in white, good luck; in black, misfortune; a murdered man, security; armed man, sorrow. 1, 19.

MARE.—To see a mare with a handsome saddle and bridle foretells that you will be married to a handsome young lady; if the mare appear old and lame, you will be connected with some lewd woman who will ruin you. 4, 17, 19, 25.

MAGGOTS.—To dream of seeing anything putrid and covered with maggots is a sign of a death; but the death may be that of your favorite dog, cat, or bird, though such a dream often foretells the death of a relative or friend. 7, 6.

MAID.—If you dream you are pleased with a pretty chambermaid, milkmaid, or any clean and nice-looking young girl whose occupation carries with it the title of maid, it is a good omen, for it predicts an excellent match and plenty of children. It also foretells, in many cases, that the dreamer will marry a rich wife. For a married woman to dream this is a sign she will have trouble with servants. 9, 11, 41.

MANNERS.—To dream of ill-mannered people who annoy you by their awkwardness and selfish conduct shows that you will shortly go on a journey and be introduced to a fool. 4, 7, 28.

MAP.—To dream of looking over a map is a sign of an agreeable surprise by the arrival of some dear friend from a distance. If a girl dreams this when her lover is away, he will return unexpectedly. 8, 5, 3.

MARKET.—To dream you are in a large market, where all kinds of meats and vegetables are sold, is a sign you will want money that it will be difficult and, perhaps, impossible to raise; it is a bad sign for tradesmen and others who have notes to pay. 11, 44.

MARRIAGE.—If any one should be so unfortunate as to dream that he or she was present at a happy and jolly wedding, it denotes that they will attend a funeral; it will not necessarily be at the burial of either of the persons you dreamed you saw married, but you will undoubtedly be called to mourn some friend or relative. To go to weddings when one is wide awake is exceedingly pleasant, but we should be careful how we dream about them. To dream of being married foretells your death. To dream you marry your sister denotes danger; a virgin, honor; a widow, losses. 4, 29.

MASK.—Hypocrisy.—16.

MASS.—To dream of hearing mass denotes high honor and a happy life. 7.

MATCH.—A sign of the acquisition of wealth. 3.

MEALS.—To dream that you are eating alone shows avarice; if in company with others, extravagance. 4, 5, 15.

MEADOW.—To dream of being in a meadow is a good sign for workingmen or shepherds; to others it signifies embarrassment in their business. 12.

MEDICINE.—To take medicine foretells poverty; to give any one medicine, gain. 7, 15.

MELONS.—To eat them, recovery from sickness. 8, 29, 35.

MIDWIFE.—To see a midwife signifies future trouble. 1, 5.

MILK.—Dreaming of milk predicts to a man the love of a lady. If a newly married lady dream that she has a full breast of milk, it is a sign that she will be happily delivered of a fine child; to an old woman it portends much money. 14.

MILL.—Not going, single and dreary life; moving, happy and eventful existence. 16, 28, 39.

MINISTER.—Benevolence. 27.

MONEY.—To find money, mourning and loss; to lose money, good business; to see it without taking it, anger and disappointment; to count it, gain. 45.

MOON.—To see the moon foretells delay in receiving money due; if its light be dim and clouded, trouble; if it be dark, misfortune; bright, high honor. 13, 29.

MOTHER.—An omen of good luck to the dreamer. To appear to live with her, security of fortune; to speak to her, good news; to dream of seeing her dead, danger to your person and property. 34, 45, 47.

MOUNTAIN.—To see a mountain shows that you will travel to distant lands. 13, 20, 16.

MOUTH.—A large mouth denotes riches; a small one, poverty; an open mouth, generosity; a mouth closed tightly, sickness. 10.

MULATTO.—To see a mulatto in sleep brings good luck; a female mulatto, dangerous sickness. 14, 15.

MURDER.—A bad dream; it signifies danger. 7, 13, 20.

MUSHROOM.—Long life. 40.

MUSIC.—Signifies consolation. 11, 13, 23.

MUSTARD.—Bad sign, except for physicians. 17, 23.

MYRTLE.—You will receive a declaration of love. 19, 21.

NAILS.—Signify an attack on your character. 11, 18, 20, 48.

NAKED.—To dream of walking about naked signifies disappointment through your friends and relations; to see a naked woman means honor and joy. 8, 76.

NAPKIN.—A white napkin denotes orderly conduct, which will bring happiness; a dirty napkin, disorderly behavior. 36, 65.

NAVEL.—To dream of having a sore navel signifies bad tidings from absent parents. 6, 12.

NEEDLES.—Deceit and mischief. 5, 40, 44, 52.

NEST.—To find a bird's-nest, signifies the augmentation of your family; to see a nest of snakes, a bad reputation. 18, 28, 45.

NEGRO.—To dream of being frightened or assaulted by a negro is a good sign, as it denotes safety; if the negro comes towards you, in a pleasant and agreeable way, it shows that you will meet with a loss or be robbed; to see a grinning, pleasant-looking negro in your dream foretells trouble through the conduct of a dependent. 14, 69.

NEST.—To find a bird's nest signifies the augmentation of your family; to see a nest of snakes, a bad reputation. 18, 28, 45.

NEW YEAR'S PRESENT.—To give one, pleasure; to receive one, embarrassment. 1, 11, 41.

NIAGARA.—As every one has heard of this great cataract, and multitudes have seen it, it is not strange that a good many people dream of going there; such a dream is a sign that you will be embarrassed in company by a sensation of some kind. 7,11, 77.

NIGHTCAP.—For a girl to dream that she forgot to take off her nightcap, but received company in it, is a sign she will be kissed by a strange gentleman, or that some stranger will be smitten by her charms; if a married woman dreams this, it foretells that her husband will be jealous of her, and, perhaps, not without cause. 17, 21.

NIGHT-OWL.—A funeral. 17, 21, 50.

NIGHTINGALE.—Light amours; to hear it sing, happiness. 10.

NOBILITY.—Should anybody be so foolish as to dream that they are created a duke, an earl, or that they have conferred upon them any patent of nobility, it is a sign of shiftlessness and poverty. If a girl dreams that a lord is in love with her, she will be apt to marry a shiftless and needy fellow. 1, 11, 41.

NODDING.—For a girl to dream that she was so sleepy in church as to nod towards the minister is a sign she will have a young parson for her husband; if a young man dreams this, he will be apt to shin up to the minister's daughter, provided his position warrants it; and if not, that he will marry a girl noted for her piety. 6, 7, 20.

NIGHTINGALE.—Light amours; to hear it sing, happiness. 10.

NOISE.—To hear a noise is a sign of joy; to make a noise, your vanity will be punished. 2, 15.

NOSE.—To dream of having a large nose denotes debauchery; crooked nose, infidelity; a nose eaten away, wantonness; if your nose appear to be larger than usual, you will become rich. 41, 57.

NUN.—For a young girl to dream of seeing a sober-looking nun, is a sign of celibacy; if she imagines she speaks to the nun, she may safely calculate on being an old maid; if a young man dreams this, it foretells that he will suspect his sweetheart of being untrue to him, and probably discard her altogether. 4, 9, 6.

NURSE.—Signifies anger. 24.

OATS.—To see a field of ripe oats, brings happiness; misfortune, to see it cut down. 1, 11, 40.

OAK.—A sign of wealth and long life. 11, 18.

OBELISK.—A sign of fame and wealth; if you mount it, great honors will be conferred upon you. 60.

OFFICE.—Benevolence. 12, 21, 24.

OFFICER.—Unpaid services. 16, 75.

OIL.—To dream it is spilled on the floor signifies damage; to spill it on yourself, profit. 6, 7, 17, 75.

ONIONS.—Foretells the discovery of secrets. 2, 9.

ORGAN.—To play it, the death of a relative. 9, 26, 70.

OWL.—An owl is the sign of crosses and grief. 26, 37, 32, 52, 65.

OX.—To see, in dreaming, an ox at labor brings joy; an ox drinking water, is a bad sign; a mad ox, quarrels; without horns, happy success; fat, fortune is near; lean, poverty; white, honor and favor; black, danger. If he walk on his hind legs, many troubles; if he jump, rivalry. It is a good sign to see one eat. 2, 4, 12, 24.

OYSTERS.—A good sign. 55.

PAINT.—To cover your own cheeks with paint signifies that you are deceitful; to paint the face of a lady shows that she deceives you. To see a painted lady warns you not to trust her. 5, 18, 23.

PALACE.—To dream of seeing a palace is a favorable sign; to live in one, good luck; if it burn, you run the risk of losing your fortune. 61.

PALM-TREE.—Signifies marriage to girls; to women, children; success and fame for men. 26, 36.

PANCAKES.—To bake them, intrigues; to eat them, indulgence in sinful pleasures. 14, 51.

PANTALOONS.—Confidence and quiet. 17, 19, 27.

PANTHER.—To dream that you see one of these animals and are terrified by it shows that you will be disgusted at the ingratitude of a friend you have served; if, in your dream, you see a tame panther and caress it, it foretells that you have some ungrateful person in your household (perhaps a servant), or else a false-hearted friend. 4, 70.

PARADE.—To dream of a parade of soldiers, and that you are delighted with the military display foretells that some one will deceive you; to a business man it is an omen of losses by bad debts or dull trade; to a young girl it foreshadows a gay but false lover; to a married woman it is a sign that her husband, though kind, will be false to his vows. 5, 29, 8.

PARASOL.—If a young woman dreams she has got a new parasol, it predicts for her a new lover; if she imagines she has broken her parasol, her lover (if she has one) will leave her; if not, then some male friend in whom she placed confidence, or derived advantage, will fail her; to a married woman, dreaming of a broken parasol is a very bad omen, as it predicts ruin to her husband. 16, 9.

PARDON.—To dream of asking pardon for an offence is a bad omen under any circumstances, as it foretells humiliation and disgrace; for a criminal to imagine, in his dream, that the Governor has pardoned him is a sign that he will not only not be pardoned, but that he will suffer much remorse and unhappiness in his imprisonment. 61.

PARTING.—To dream of parting from friends with regret is a sign of disappointment; if a young girl dreams that her lover is going away anywhere, and she feels bad when he takes his leave, it predicts that he will not "go raving distracted with delight" the next time he comes to see her, and she will consequently be disappointed at his supposed coolness; hut all this may not amount to anything more than to make her feel bad for the time being. 8, 2, 1.

PAWNBROKER.—Some honorable and profitable office. 3, 16.

PARROT.—To dream that you are pleased with the chattering of one of these birds is a sign that some deceitful person will flatter you; if an engaged young girl has such a dream, she should look sharp to the antecedents of her lover before marriage, as it is ten to one that he is not worthy of her confidence; the dream may, however, point to some other flatterer. 38, 33, 51.

PEACOCK.—If a man dream he sees one, he will marry a beautiful woman; if a woman, she will marry a handsome man. 5, 29.

PEARL.—Solitude and tears. 9.

PEARS.—Ripe and mellow pears, give joy and pleasure; choke-pears, bring misery and pain. 12, 21, 35, 53.

PEAS.—To dream of eating peas brings fortune and good business prospects. 47.

PENKNIFE.—Infidelity in the married life. 22.

PEPPER.—Avarice. 8.

PIANO.—To dream of hearing pleasant and lively tunes played on the piano is a sign of thrift and domestic happiness; but if you dream of buying, or that any one presents you with a piano, it foreshadows poverty; it is a bad omen for a girl to dream she has got a beautiful new piano. 26, 70.

PICKLES.—If a girl dreams of eating pickles, it is a sign some old bachelor will kiss her; if a young man dreams of pickled cucumbers, he will be beloved by a maid older than himself, and probably of a sour and crabbed temper. 9, 8.

PICNIC.—For a young man to dream of going with a picnic party into the woods is a sign that some silly girl will fall in love with him; if a young girl dreams this, some vain fellow will probably pay her attentions and compliments merely to gratify his own vanity. 9, 16.

PIGS.—Signify that there are sluggards who wish to live at your expense. 4, 50, 70.

PINS.—Slight quarrels. 46.

PIPE.—To break one, a quarrel; to smoke one, success. 18.

PITCHER.—Bankruptcy through your own carelessness. 18.

PINEAPPLE.—To dream of this fruit is a sign of gold; if you see an abundance of it, you will receive plenty of gold soon after; a young girl who dreams of pineapples will probably get a rich husband. 11, 42.

PISTOL.—To dream of arming yourself with a pistol foretells that you will lose caste, and, perhaps, become poor; if a girl dreams that her lover carries a pistol, she may be sure that he is below her in social life, and therefore an unpropitious or unsuitable match. 34, 11.

PHEASANT.—Health and riches. 31.

PLAINS.—To dream of being on a beautiful plain, happiness. 66, 71.

PLAYING BALL.—Dreaming of playing ball, or seeing it played, foretells the speedy receipt of money; to see the ball roll about signifies delay in its reception. 8, 9, 16.

PLOUGH.—To dream of a plough coming towards you denotes success in your enterprises; if going from you, embarrassments in business. 1, 27, 53.

PLUMS.—To see plums, care; to eat them, disappointment; plums out of season indicate misfortune. 14, 57.

POLICE OFFICER.—Such a dream should teach you to beware of false friends. 1, 2, 5, 31.

POND.—To dream of seeing a pond of clear water foretells friendship and wealth; if the water be muddy, sorrow and poverty; filled with large fish, an increase of property; dead fish in the pond signify theft and bankruptcy. 3, 33, 51.

POPE.—Happiness in futurity. 38.

PORT.—To see a seaport, gain, with pleasant tidings. 11, 49.

PORTRAIT.—Long life to one who dreams of his own portrait; but treachery to one who receives his portrait. 18, 19, 29.

POST.—Obstacles to success. 16, 18.

PRAISE.—To praise some one, useless lies; to be praised, impudent flattery. 57, 62.

PRESENTS.—To receive them from a distinguished person denotes change of fortune for the better; a present from a man signifies good advice; from a female, love; from a boy, trouble; to give a present shows ingratitude. 42, 44, 46.

PRESERVES.—To make or eat them foretells the acquisition of much money. 14,50.

PRIEST.—To see a priest in your dream denotes sickness; if the priest be clad in his robes, you will make confession of your faults. 5, 11, 40.

PRISON.—To dream of entering a prison, happiness; to remain in it, consolation; to leave it, danger. 7, 27.

PROMENADE.—To be promenading signifies joy, followed by sorrow. 13, 76.

PROSTITUTE.—For a young man to dream of associating with prostitutes is a sign of poverty and disgrace; if he dreams of seeing these girls anywhere, it foretells misfortune or bad luck; for a girl to dream of them is a sign that her chastity is in danger. 38, 6.

PRUDE.—To dream that you are prudish signifies that you are the reverse. 21, 40.

PSALM.—To be singing psalms indicates trouble in business. 50, 56, 69.

PYRAMIDS.—To dream of seeing pyramids denotes the acquisition of honor and wealth; to stand on one brings high station in society. 65.

QUAIL.—Bad tidings. 2, 6, 11.

QUARREL.—To quarrel with your sweetheart denotes your speedy union together; with a friend, the loss of money, 33, 47.

RABBIT.—To dream of a black rabbit denotes some bad accident; a white one, success. To eat one, good health. 4, 10,12.

RAIN.—If it rains lightly and unaccompanied by wind it is a good dream for workingmen. To dream of a storm is bad for men in business. For the poor man it is a sign of better fortune. 43, 45.

RAGS.—Denotes shame and misery; to pick them, great pain. 24, 29, 37.

RAINBOW.—To dream of seeing a rainbow in the West is a good sign for the poor and sick; in the East, a good omen for the rich. If it is overhead, look for misery and the death of some one you love. 10, 17, 70.

RAFFLE.—Raffling in your dream is the same as gambling; it foretells poverty and disgrace; to dream of raffling for poultry is a sign that your family (if you have one) will want bread; if you are single, it shows that you will be apt to get seedy and loaferish. 11, 34.

RAFT.—To dream of seeing a raft foretells a journey—the longer the raft, the more extensive the line of travel; if you dream of sailing on a raft, it is a sign you will travel, with good success, in distant countries. 6, 32.

RAGE.—If you dream that you are in a great rage in consequence of a mishap, or disagreeable event, it is a sign that some pleasant episode in connection therewith will occur to put you in an excellent humor, as such dreams work contrariwise. 37, 63.

RAILROAD.—To dream of travelling by railroad foretells to people who keep house that they will break up their establishment; to young persons it indicates the loss of their home; to lovers it is a sign that if they marry they will not keep house long, if at all. 8, 11, 5.

RAINBOW.—It is an excellent dream to imagine you see a brilliant rainbow—the brighter the better; it denotes health and general prosperity; to lovers it foretells a happy marriage and riches. A young girl who dreams of a rainbow will either get an agreeable lover or a present. 13, 14.

RAKING.—For a girl to dream of raking newly-mown hay is a sign she will be married before the hay is eaten; young fellows who dream of raking hay with their sweethearts had better get ready their necks for the matrimonial noose, as they are past praying for. 22, 32.

RAM.—If it butt you, it signifies loss of property. 4, 20.

RATS.—Secret enemies. 4, 16, 32.

RAVEN.—To see one, adultery and misfortune. 2, 3, 9.

RAYS.—To have a crown of rays around your head is a very favorable sign. If you see rays around the head of an enemy, he will defeat you; if you see rays around the head of a woman, make love to her and you will succeed in your desires. 42, 61.

REPAIRING.—If you dream of repairing a house it foretells sickness; but if you imagine that some needed repairs are already done, when in fact they are not, it is a sign that you will have a piece of good luck in connection with that house; to dream that a house is pulled to pieces for repairs foretells the death of the master of it. 9, 4.

REPRIEVE.—If a criminal under sentence of death dreams of a reprieve or pardon, he may make up his mind that it is all over with him; and if any friend who is interested in his fate dreams this, it amounts to about the same thing. 6, 11, 3.

REPTILE.—To dream of any animal that is called a reptile, such as snakes, toads, alligators, and the like, is a sign of a quarrel; if you imagine you are bitten, it shows that you will come out second best, or badly injured either in person or reputation. If a girl dreams of a reptile, let her look sharp that her lover don't play her false. 39, 8.

RESCUE.—If you dream of rescuing any one from peril, it is a sign you will rise in the world, either by means of increased wealth or new honors; to dream that you are rescued from drowning, or from any other mode of death, shows that you will go into some successful business speculation with a partner. To lovers such a dream foretells a speedy and happy union. 3, 86.

RESIGN.—If a person who holds an office, or a trust of any kind, dreams of resigning, it is a sign of advancement; to any one who cannot be advanced, it shows that he will rise above his present position in society. 19, 20.

RESUSCITATE.—To dream of resuscitating a drowned person foretells that you will engage in some enterprise that attracts public attention; if the person thus brought to life is a female, it shadows forth marriage with a lady of public fame. 15.

RETURN.—If a person who is travelling or sojourning abroad dreams of returning home, it is a sign he will hear bad news; to dream of returning from a journey before you have started to go on it foretells that you will suffer from a serious accident should you go. If a girl dreams that her lover returns after starting to go home, it foreshadows his death. 38, 6.

RIBS.—To dream of having the ribs broken, quarrel between husband and wife. 27.

RICE.—Denotes abundance, and increased happiness. 17, 71.

RIDER.—A good sign to one who never rides on horseback; to fall from a horse, signifies loss. 6, 27.

RING.—To receive one, friendship; to give a ring, confidence. For a lady to dream that a gentleman presents her with a ring, or that she has a ring belonging to a gentleman, is a sign of a wedding; if a young man dreams that he has got a lady's ring, the omen is similar;

to dream of finding a ring foretells that the person finding it will marry within a year. 44, 11.

RIOT.—To dream of a public tumult or riot is a sign of scarcity and bad crops to farmers, and dull business to tradesmen and mechanics; if any friend or relative is injured in the riot, you or they will probably suffer from misfortune; but if they are successful and pacify the crowd, it foretells that you will overcome your difficulties. 39, 61.

RIVAL.—For a lover to dream that he has a rival who annoys him is a sign that he is in high favor with his sweetheart; such a dream to a young lady has a similar omen, and she has only to name the happy day to settle the matter to her mind. 14, 15.

RIVER.—To dream of swimming in a river indicates that danger is nigh; to be in a rapid river and not able help yourself shows sickness, danger, and long lawsuits. To see a small, clear river signifies to a man that he will marry a neat and pretty wife; to a maiden this dream portends the realizing of her desires. To see a clear river flowing through your chamber shows that you will be befriended by some person of great influence. If the stream appears muddy and dull, it brings quarrelling and disturbance. 17, 40, 60.

ROAD.—To be travelling on a good and straight road denotes good luck; if it be uneven and muddy, you will have many obstacles to contend with; if it be very bad, some of those you deal with will cheat you. 39.

ROBBERS.—To dream of being attacked by robbers shows loss of money or friends. 19, 56.

ROBIN.—To dream of seeing robins around your house is a good omen, as it foretells abundance to farmers and success to any one; if you do not see them, but hear them trilling, it foreshadows sickness and, perhaps, death. 6, 3.

ROCKET.—To dream of seeing rockets flying in the air foretells joy and gladness at some event about to happen; to married people it denotes the birth of a child, or the marriage of a daughter, if they have one old enough. If a young girl dreams of seeing a rocket, she needn't trouble herself further, as her speedy marriage is certain. 8, 11.

ROCKING-CHAIR.—You will obtain a good situation. 25.

ROCKS.—If you are on them, prepare for trouble; if you come down from them, you will find friends. 21, 30, 36.

ROOSTER.—If a girl dreams of hearing a cock crow, it foretells that she will soon have a new lover; if a lover dreams this, it is a sign that he has a formidable rival; if a married man or woman dreams of roosters, it shows that some outsider is enamored of the wife. 34.

ROSEMARY.—To see it, a good reputation; to smell it mourning. 27, 30,43.

ROSES.—To see them, or to hold them in the hand, in their season, is an excellent dream; out of season, it is a bad sign. 3, 8, 13, 14, 24.

RUINS.—To see them denotes repentance. 1.

RUN.—It is a good sign to dream of running. To run naked denotes infidelity in marriage; to run after an enemy, victory; to see many people running signifies quarrels. 6, 15, 40.

SALAD.—Sickness, if it be eaten. 9, 27.

SAND.—Instability. 8, 16, 24.

SAUSAGES.—To dream of making sausages predicts quarrels; to eat them, love to the young, and health to old people. 4, 32, 40.

SCALES.—Denote arrest, and appearance before a court. 7, 59, 67.

SCAFFOLD.—Dangerous speculations. 45.

SCHOOL.—To dream of being in one, an increase of knowledge; to go into one, modesty; to bring your children into school shows that you will set them a good example. 15, 17, 39, 54.

SCISSORS.—Signify quarrels between lovers; disputes of married couples, and trouble in business. 6, 18, 36.

SCORPION.—Loss by secret enemies. 9, 23.

SCYTHE.—Always a bad sign. 33, 44.

SHEEP.—To see them is a sign of consolation; if you see them sleeping or dead, you will have sorrow. To carry one signifies great luck; to hear them bleat, damage and loss. A sign of good luck to be surrounded by many sheep. To kill one, or to see them killed, great sorrow. 4, 45, 56, 68.

SHELL.—An empty shell denotes loss of time and money; a full one, success. 36.

SHEPHERD.—The appearance of one warns you to be careful in what you undertake. 7, 14, 21.

SHIRT.—To dream of wearing a clean shirt foretells happiness; if the shirt be torn, your hopes will be disappointed. 43, 54.

SHIP.—To dream you are sailing in a ship, in fair weather, pleasure and security in business; if it be stormy, bad fortune. To be in danger of shipwreck shows insecurity of property; but to a prisoner it indicates speedy release. The tackle and sails of a ship foretells heavy losses from debtors and agents. 11, 22, 23.

SHOES.—To dream of new shoes, fortune; to lose your shoes, poverty. 5, 9, 16, 55.

SHOOT.—To see a person shooting indicates some disagreeable event; if you shoot yourself, unexpected misfortune. 8, 53, 57.

SHOULDER.—Large, wealth; dislocated, bad news; fleshy, good luck. 59, 66.

SHOWBILLS.—To dream of putting one on a wall predicts that some injury will befall you. To read one shows that you will fail in receiving a reward for your labors. 39, 41, 53.

SICKNESS.—Loneliness and imprisonment. 26, 31, 14, 67, 69.

SILK.—Foretells abundance. 31, 62.

SILVERWARE.—To buy it, misfortune; to sell it, good luck, and great success in what you undertake. 12, 15, 20, 39.

SINGING.—For a man to dream of singing brings hope; to a woman, sorrow. 24.

SKY.—A clear sky denotes a marriage, speedy and happy; a red sky, increase of wealth; if you ascend into the sky, you may look for much honor; a cloudy sky, shows misfortune. 22, 24.

SLAUGHTER-HOUSE.—To dream of being in an empty slaughter-house shows that you are in danger, but can avoid it by precaution. To see animals slaughtered is a good sign, if the blood flow freely; if the blood does not flow, you will meet with some accident. 13, 26, 39.

SLEEP.—To dream that you sleep with a person of the opposite sex signifies hindrance in your projects; with a person of the same sex, perplexing events. If a man sleep with an ugly woman, it means mischief to himself; with a melancholy-looking woman, dangerous sickness; with a handsome woman, treachery. For a woman to sleep with her absent husband, it denotes bad news. To sleep with your wife, pleasure; with your mother, good business; with your daughter, scandal; with your sister, departure; with a fashionable woman, success. 14, 28, 56.

SLEEPLESSNESS.—To dream that you cannot sleep is a sign of mourning. 15, 30.

SMOKE.—Prudery and vanity. 12, 24, 49.

SNAKE.—A snake signifies injury by the malice of a man, or treachery from a woman. To kill one, victory. Sickness and ill-fortune to dream of one twining around you. 16, 32, 49, 64.

SNEEZE.—To sneeze, long life. 21, 42.

SNOW.—To see it fall, obstacles. 42, 44, 46, 62.

SOAP.—Signifies trouble in business, but it will soon depart. 8, 18, 33, 66, 74.

SOCIETY.—To dream of being in the company of distinguished persons foretells honor and happiness. 23, 46, 77.

SOMNAMBULIST.—To dream of walking in sleep, shows sickness and fever. 18, 36, 51.

SORES.—To have the arm full of sores shows ill success in business. 22, 44, 67.

SORROW.—To feel much sorrow in a dream means unexpected joy. 27, 31.

SPECTRE.—White, brings joy, pleasure, and good fortune; black, pain and trouble. 21, 30, 35.

SPIDER.—To dream that a spider looks at you foretells that you will be the victim of treachery. To kill a spider, sorrow and ill luck. 54, 75.

SPONGE.—Avarice and bad faith. 26.

SPRING.—A spring of gushing water signifies wealth and honor; a spring from which water does not flow, poverty and sickness. 12, 14.

SPY.—Shows servitude. 41, 65.

STABLE.—Denotes hospitality and good entertainment. 22, 44.

STAGE-COACH.—To dream of riding in one signifies losses through delays; if you run after one, you will be out of employment for a long season; to see one pass, will rid you of troublesome friends. If you are in a stage-coach, and it turns over without injuring; you, you will be lucky in your speculations; if you dream you are killed by the fall, you must expect misfortune. 51, 57, 75.

STARS.—Brightly shining, show happy success; dim, trouble; seen over a house, danger of death in the family; a star falling from heaven, quarrels with a friend. 19, 20.

STEEL.—To break a piece in a dream shows that, you will overcome your enemies; if you only touch it, your position in life is secure; if you try to bend it and cannot, you will meet with many serious accidents. 11, 18.

STILTS.—To dream of being mounted on stilts denotes that you are puffed up with vain pride. 14, 21.

STICK.—To hold a stick foretells mourning; to use it as a prop, instability of fortune; to beat any one with it shows you are charitable; to receive a beating with one predicts trouble and lawsuits. 41, 56.

STIRRUP.—Signifies a journey. 47.

STOCKINGS.—To dream of cotton stockings foretells moderate happiness; of silk, poverty. To take them off denotes the reception of money. Stockings with holes in them signify the loss of property. 29, 35, 56, 66.

STONES.—Anger and quarrels. 5, 42.

STOOL.—Honor. 68.

STORK.—Dreamed of in summer, beware of thieves; in winter it means bad weather and change of residence. 2, 14, 43.

STORM.—Great danger. 4, 24.

STOVE.—A sign of wealth, if there there be a fire in it; but if cold, a sign of poverty. 17.

STRANGLE.—To dream of strangling any one predicts victory over enemies; to strangle one's self by eating shows sickness, caused by too much indulgence. 23, 32, 44.

STRAW.—A bundle of straw denotes abundance; if scattered about, poverty. 13, 20.

STRAW-HAT.—Modesty. 1, 8, 71.

STRUGGLE.—To dream of struggling in death denotes the enjoyment of good health; to see a friend in the pangs of death shows that he is well and happy; to see a woman die means loss of property. 17, 34, 71.

STUDY.—Tranquil and lasting happiness. 57, 73.

STUTTER.—To dream of stuttering shows resolution. 8, 41, 50.

SUICIDE.—To dream of committing suicide shows that your mind is disordered. 3, 9, 29, 37, 73.

SUN-DIAL.—Take heed how you spend your time. 49, 66.

SUN.—To dream of seeing the sun rise brings good news and luck; the setting sun, misfortune; if its disc be dim, personal danger; with brilliant face, glory and fame; a red sun, misfortune. The conjunction of the sun and moon portends a great war. 7, 29.

SURGEON.—An unexpected event. 10.

SUSPENDERS.—To wear them, precaution; to take them off, some disagreeable event. 11, 31, 63.

SWALLOW.—Good news. 2, 22, 25, 50, 75.

SWAMP.—To dream of falling into one, poverty. 70.

SWAN.—A white swan signifies riches; a black one, domestic sorrow. Its song denotes death. 2, 27, 54.

SWEEP.—To dream of sweeping one's room, good luck in business; to sweep a room, merited confidence; a cellar, misfortune. 24, 42, 55.

SWORD.—To dream of seeing a sword is a prediction of treachery. To wear one signifies the possession of power; to be beat with one, misfortune and disgrace. 1, 9, 25, 31.

TALKING.—If you dream that you talk much, you will be exposed to some malicious plans; if you hear much talking around you, be careful of your neighbors. 48, 57.

TEARS.—Consolation. 43, 50, 57.

TEN-PINS.—To dream of playing ten-pins foretells disgrace; if the centre pin falls, one of the players will die; if many pins fall, all of the players will suffer loss. 10, 40, 48, 67.

THIGH.—For a man to dream of having a broken thigh shows loss of goods sent to distant parts; if a young girl dream it, she will marry a stranger and live far away from her relatives; widowhood for a woman. If a man see the white and handsome thigh of a woman, he will be always fortunate. 41, 65, 67.

THIRST.—To feel thirst, ambitious, but unsuccessful; if quenched, riches. 39, 65.

THISTLE.—To cut them signifies laziness; to be pricked by them, serious injury. 14, 44, 62.

TRAVEL.—On foot, denotes embarassments and delays in what you undertake or hope for; on horseback, good fortune; in a wagon, change of fortune for the better. 6, 42, 63.

TRICKS.—To dream a lady plays you tricks indicates that you will lose your love. 17.

TRIUMPHAL ARCH.—Honor and high office. 49, 55, 56.

TRUNK.—A full trunk shows the necessity of economy; an empty one signifies that you may expect to receive money. 38, 68.

TWINS.—To dream of having twins brings good news. 5, 47, 55, 58.

TUB.—If it be filled with water, you have evil to fear; an empty tub signifies trouble; and to run against one, sorrow. 43, 59.

TUMOUR.—The bankruptcy of some one who owes you money. 4, 32.

TURNIP.—The discovery of secrets and domestic quarrels. 28, 39, 40, 64.

UNDRESS.—To see your wife undress signifies wantonness; to undress in the presence of others, slander; to undress in your room alone, the discovery of secrets. 2, 25, 30.

UMBRELLA.—Momentary good fortune. 55, 77.

VAULT.—An unexpected estate will fall to you if you dream of a vault. 67, 76.

VEGETABLE.—To dream of eating vegetables, misfortune. 24, 48.

VEIL.—Pretended modesty. 12.

VELVET.—Wealth and power. 10, 73.

VILLAGE.—To see, loss of office; a burning village, great honor. 3, 9, 36, 37.

VINE.—A sign of abundance. 5, 20, 25, 31.

VINEYARD.—A very good sign. 6, 36.

VINEGAR.—Dreaming of red vinegar signifies that somebody will insult you; white vinegar indicates that your friends will be injured. To drink vinegar is the sign of domestic dissensions. 13, 61, 66, 71.

VIOLET.—To see one in season, means happiness in love; out of season, loss of property, friends, or mistress. 9, 45.

VISIT.—If you dream of receiving a visit, you will undertake some enterprise at present unthought of. To pay a visit foretells some great loss. To be visited by a physician brings great profit. 4, 16, 64.

WALL.—If it stands in your way, embarrassments; if you jump over it, joy. 14.

WASHING.—To be washing signifies a happy event. 24, 28, 30, 50.

WASPS.—To be stung by one, in a dream, much trouble. 66.

WATCH.—To dream of having a watch is a warning to be careful how you spend your time. 22, 33, 60, 70.

WATCHMAN.—To dream of calling in one gives confidence; to see a person taken to prison by a watchman shows that you must be careful in conducting your business. If the watchman take hold of you, it is a very good sign. To see many watchmen together signifies the loss of money. 1, 9, 23.

WAX.—Denotes weakness of character. 24, 35.

WAX-CANDLE.—To dream of seeing a wax-candle burning signifies, to a pregnant woman, a speedy and happy delivery; many wax candles, sudden death of a relative. 25, 36.

WAR.—Signifies trouble and danger. To dream you go to war foretells good news. 2, 22, 56.

WALKING.—To be fatigued in walking denotes much trouble; to be walking in dirty places shows infidelity in the married state. 18, 49, 63.

WAVES.—Signify to a maiden you will receive the attentions of a dishonest lover. 7, 9, 63.

WASTE-PLACES.—Denote some dangerous enterprise. 3, 14, 19, 33.

WALNUTS.—Signify the fulfilment of your most sanguine wishes. 8 to 78 combination.

WAGES.—Denote bad temper and disappointment. 4, 26, 54.

WAGON.—To dream of a wagon you will surely have some good fortune. 4, 11, 44.

WAITER.—Signifies dishonest servants. 40, 48, 50.

WANDERING.—To dream of wandering about, signifies loss of goods by fire. To dream of a wanderer denotes shame. 18, 21, 63.

WANT.—To dream you are in want signifies riches. 1, 6, 69.

WARMING-PAN.—Denotes abundance. 1, 50, 72.

WART.—To dream your hands are full of warts shows you must be careful in conducting your business. 5, 9, 14.

WEATHERCOCK.—A changeable mind. 1, 12.

WEDDING.—A sign of a funeral; to dance at a wedding, sickness. 6, 28, 43, 73.

WEEPING.—To dream one weeps and grieves is a sure sign of pleasure. 2, 22, 33.

WEIGHING.—To dream you are engaged in weighing you will overcome your difficulty. 1, 50, 61.

WELL.—A well full of clear sparkling water denotes successful speculation; an overflowing well, losses. 20, 31.

WHEEL.—Is ominous of evil. To dream of a wheelwright denotes sorrow, followed by joy. 1, 24, 50.

WHITE WAX.—A sign of grief to all but mariners. 8, 30, 40.

WHITE LEAD.—Denotes quarrels. 43, 69, 78.

WHALE.—Some danger threatens you. 27, 38,78,

WILD BEAST.—Of any kind, signifies the protection and favor of persons of distinction. 3, 4, 28.

WILL.—A very bad sign. 74, 78.

WIG.—Beware of a neglected cold or cough. 11, 31, 57, 63.

WIND.—Fright. 5, 20, 31, 75.

WINDOWS.—To dream that you throw yourself out shows you will meet with some accident, or lose a lawsuit you expected to gain. If you step through a window, some one will injure you. An open window signifies that you are favored by persons of distinction; a window closed means embarrassments. 30, 65, 69.

WINE.—To dream of drinking good wine shows power and fortune; wine and water, bad health; white wine, pleasure trips; if the wine be not clear, it signifies wealth; to see it flow, the spilling of blood. To get drunk from good wine indicates office and fortune. 10, 29, 48.

WIND.—To dream you hear the wind blow denotes sickness. To be caught in a gust of wind denotes fright. To dream of a windmill, you will experience some loss. 1, 5, 42.

WIDOW.—To dream of a widow signifies a reward; to dream you are a widow portends death or disappointment. To dream of a widower denotes strife and quarrels. 15, 50, 75.

WOLF.—To dream of seeing a wolf shows an avaricious and hard-hearted neighbor; to conquer a wolf signifies that you will overthrow some one who has all the bad qualities of a wolf. 4, 15, 53.

WOODS.—To dream of hiding yourself in the woods shows you are in danger. 4, 43, 58.

WOODYARD.—To be in one, happy change of fortune; if you own one, good luck and abundance. 26, 37.

WORMS.—You will despise your friends. 6, 8, 44, 60.

WORMWOOD.—Sorrow, followed by joy. 11, 32.

WOUND.—To dream of being wounded by a dagger signifies benevolence; a wound made by an unknown person denotes much trouble; by a wolf, infidelity in marriage; if the wound heals, you will be the victim of ingratitude. To wound another person will subject you to unjust suspicion. 6, 21,32.

WOOL.—To dream you are buying wool foretells you will marry your present lover. To dream you sell wool is ominous of sickness. To dream of a wood-dealer denotes affluence. 64, 67, 69.

WRITE.—To dream of writing a letter foretells good news; a bill, an accusation. 43, 44, 55, 59.

YACHT.—Signifies distress; to the sailor, a stormy voyage. 1, 11, 33, 47.

YARD.—Denotes loss of business. 4, 8, 12.

YARN.—Is ominous of disgrace. 4, 44, 50.

YEAST.—Foretells sickness and vexation. 2, 4, 68.

YEOMAN.—Is the forerunner of evil. 1, 2, 60.

YEW-TREE.—To dream of a yew-tree, the dreamer will arrive at some great honor and receive a legacy from a relative. 4, 6, 11, 44, 66.

YOUNG.—To fancy yourself young denotes that some unexpected news will reach you. 1, 10, 11, 12.

YOUTH.—For a woman to dream her youth restored, she will have a loving and true husband. 11, 12, 21, 56.

YOUNG MAN.—Augurs but little good to the dreamer. 27, 36, 72.

ZEBRA.—4, 11, 44.

ZODIAC.—To dream of the twelve signs of the Zodiac denotes that a man will become popular and be a great traveller. 17, 71, 75, 69, 70.

COMBINATION TABLE

		Saddles.	Gigs.	Horses.
2	Numbers make	1	0	0
3	" "	3	1	0
4	" "	6	4	1
5	" "	10	10	4
6	" "	15	20	15
7	" "	21	35	35
8	" "	28	56	70
9	" "	36	84	126
10	" "	45	120	210
11	" "	55	165	330
12	" "	66	220	495
13	" "	78	286	715
14	" "	91	364	1001
15	" "	105	455	1365
16	" "	120	560	1820
17	" "	136	680	2380
18	" "	153	816	3060
19	" "	171	969	3876
20	" "	190	1140	4845
21	" "	210	1330	5985

22	" "	231	1540	7315
23	" "	253	1771	8855
24	" "	276	2024	10626
25	" "	300	2300	12650

WHEN TO PLAY GIGS.

It is a good time to play a Gig when the numbers are running.

Always arrange it so as to make your play over in the night drawings.

Numbers for the days of the month and classes:

Play						
1	on the	4th	and	20th	of the month.
3	"	10th			"
4	"	10th			"
6	"	4th	and	17th	"
9	"	20th			"
10	"	11th			"
11	"	10th			"
14	"	9th	and	25th	"
15	"	8th			"
17	"	4th	and	6th	"
22	"	7th			"
23	"	13th			"
31	"	5th			"
41	"	15th			"
44	"	11th	and	13th	"

45   "   20th   "

PLAYING GIGS.

—

GOOD COMBINATIONS TO PLAY.

—

1, 10, 11, 42, 69.

1, 10, 42, 44, 69.

6, 9, 10, 11, 17, 44, 71.

6, 10, 11, 44, 71.

39, 50, 61, 74.

4, 39, 74, 76.

10, 51, 61, 70, 74.

1, 10, 61, 64, 66.

44, 66, 68, 70, 75.

5, 25, 55, 65.

4, 14, 56, 60.

2, 12, 24, 72, 75.

11, 44, 66, 77.

2, 3, 4, 8, 50.

8, 46, 50, 59.

3, 45, 55, 60.

3, 25, 45, 55.

3, 25, 42, 55.

1, 2, 16, 40, 44.

12, 24, 48, 62, 63.

17, 39, 47, 50.

8, 24, 25, 33, 46.

13, 16, 53, 72, 73.

17, 30, 44, 73.

30, 72, 73, 75.

9, 15, 17, 47.

39, 46, 50, 61.

15, 27, 66, 68.

32, 33, 77, 78.

1, 6, 16, 61.

5, 8, 10, 25, 50.

4, 11, 14, 33, 44.

8, 13, 33, 54, 66.

6, 11, 25, 28, 32.

7, 11, 12, 16, 28.

3, 11, 33, 19, 66.

9, 19, 29, 33, 44.

3, 6, 9, 60, 66.

8, 12, 18, 20, 28.

16, 38, 49, 52, 64.

19, 28, 33, 54, 65.

18, 25, 28, 44, 64.

19, 33, 49, 52, 69.

13, 29, 39, 44, 66.

4, 22, 69, 75, 77.

7, 11, 54, 59, 75.

7, 22, 49, 64.

12, 17, 21, 38, 51.

2, 22, 56, 77.

3, 5, 11, 29.

1, 8, 16, 17.

4, 21, 32, 44.

14, 24, 36, 65.

17, 19, 26, 47.

2, 22, 25, 50, 75.

18, 49, 57, 70.

20, 25, 31, 60.

8, 39, 65, 66.

DOMINOES.

Lay them with their faces on the table and shuffle them; then draw one and see the number, which has its meaning as follows:

DOUBLE-SIX.—Receiving a handsome sum of money.

SIX-FIVE.—Going to a public amusement.

SIX-FOUR.—Law-suits

SIX-THREE.—Ride in a coach.

SIX-TWO.—Present of clothing.

SIX-ONE.—You will soon perform a friendly action.

SIX-BLANK.—Guard against scandal, or you will suffer by your inattention.

DOUBLE-FIVE.—A new abode to your advantage.

FIVE-FOUR.—A fortunate speculation.

FIVE-THREE.—A visit from a superior.

FIVE-TWO.—A water party.

FIVE-ONE.—A love intrigue.

FIVE-BLANK.—A funeral, but not of a relation.

DOUBLE-FOUR.—Drinking liquor at a distance.

FOUR-THREE.—A false alarm at your house.

FOUR-TWO.—Beware of thieves or swindlers. Ladies, take notice of this; it means more than it says.

FOUR-ONE.—Trouble from creditors.

FOUR-BLANK.—Receive a letter from an angry friend.

DOUBLE-THREE.—Sudden wedding, at which you will be vexed.

THREE-TWO.—Buy no lottery tickets, nor enter into any game of chance, or you will lose.

THREE-ONE.—A great discovery at hand.

THREE-BLANK.—An illegitimate child.

DOUBLE-TWO.—You will be plagued by a jealous partner.

TWO-ONE.—You will mortgage or pledge some property very soon.

Double-one.—You will find something to your advantage in the street or road.

ONE-BLANK.—You are being closely watched by one whom you little expect.

DOUBLE-BLANK.—The worst presage in all the set of dominoes; you will soon meet trouble from a quarter from which you are quite unprepared.

It is useless for any person to draw more than three dominoes at one time of trial, or in one and the same month, as they will only deceive themselves; shuffle the dominoes each time of choosing; to draw the same dominoe twice makes the answer stronger.

AUGURY BY DICE

Take three dice, shake them well in the box with your left hand, and then cast them out on a board or table, on which you had previously drawn a circle with chalk, but never throw on a Monday or Wednesday.

THREE.—A pleasing surprise

FOUR.—A disagreeable one.

FIVE.—A stranger who will prove a friend.

SIX.—Loss of property.

SEVEN.—Undeserved scandal.

EIGHT.—Merited reproach.

NINE.—A wedding.

TEN.—A christening, at which some important event will occur to you.

ELEVEN.—A death that concerns you.

TWELVE.—A letter speedily.

THIRTEEN.—Tears and sighs.

FOURTEEN.—A new admirer.

Fifteen.—Beware that you are not drawn into some trouble or plot.

SIXTEEN.—A pleasant journey.

SEVENTEEN.—You will either be on the water, or have dealings with those belonging to it, to your advantage.

EIGHTEEN.—A great profit, rise in life, or some most desirable good will happen almost immediately; for the answers to the dice are always fulfilled within nine days.

To show the same number twice at one trial shows news from abroad, be the number what it may. If the dice roll over the circle, the number thrown goes for nothing, but the occurrence shows sharp words, and, if they fall to the floor, it is blows; in throwing out the dice, if one remains on the top of the other, it is a present, of which I would have the females take care.

To Know What Fortune Your Future Husband Will Have.

Take a walnut, a hazel-nut, and nutmeg; grate them together, and mix them with butter and sugar, and make them up into small pills, of which exactly nine must be taken on going to bed; and according to her dreams, so will be the state of the person she will marry. If a gentleman, of riches; if a clergyman, of white linen; if a lawyer, of darkness; if a tradesman, of odd noises and tumults; If a soldier or sailor, of thunder and lightning; if a servant, of rain.

CURIOUS
Traditional Observations.

—

It is not good for a maiden to marry in colors, or a widow in white; yet let her, by all means, avoid green or yellow and the 13th of the month.

To see a flight of birds as you go to the church on your nuptial day foretells many children. To meet a funeral at the time is ominous of speedy separation.

The sun to emerge suddenly from behind a cloud and shine on the altar as the nuptials are celebrating is a sure omen of prosperity and connubial love.

It is unlucky to pick up an odd glove in the street; you had better pass it.

Never tell a dream till you have broke your fast; if you have the same dream repeated twice or thrice, attend to it; it must have more than common meaning.

To Find Out the Two First Letters of
a Wife's or Husband's Name.

Take a small Bible and the key of your front street-door, and having opened to Solomon's Songs, chapter 8, verses 6 and 7, place the wards of the key on these two verses, and let the bow of the key be about an inch out of the top of the Bible; then shut the book and tie it round with your garter, so as the key will not move, and the person who wishes to know his or her future husband or wife's signature must suspend the Bible by putting the middle finger of the right hand under the bow of the key, and the other person in like manner on the other side of the bow of the key, who must repeat the following verses, after the other person's saying the alphabet, one letter to each time repeating them. It must be observed that you mention to the person who repeats the verses, before you begin, which you intend to try first, whether surname or Christian name; and take care to hold the Bible steady, and when you arrive at the appointed letter, the book will turn round under your finger, and that you will find to be the first letter of your intended's name.

SOLOMON'S SONGS, VIII. 6, 7:

"Set me as a seal upon thine heart, as a seal upon thine arm; for love is strong as death, jealousy is cruel as the grave; the coals thereof are coals of fire, which hath a most vehement flame.

"Many waters cannot quench love, neither can the floods drown it; if a man would give all the substance of Iris house for love, it would utterly be contemned."

Several Queries Resolved in Matters of Love and Business by Throwing the Die, or Pricking at a Figure, after the Rules of the Following Table:

A	1	2	3	4	5	6
B	1	2	3	4	5	6
C	1	2	3	4	5	6
D	1	2	3	4	5	6
E	1	2	3	4	5	6

What number you throw, go to that, or else what number or letter you prick upon, they being covered with a piece of paper, through which you must prick.

As to what kind of a Husband a Widow or Maid shall have.

1. A handsome youth, be sure, you'll have,
   Brown-hair'd, high-nos'd; he'll keep thee brave.
2. A man unto thy lot will fall,
   Straight, but neither short nor tall.
3. An honest tradesman is thy lot;
   When he proffers, slight him not.
4. Fair, ruddy, bushy-haired is thy love,
   He'll keep thee well, and call thee still his dove.
5. A widower, though rich, thou'lt marry,
   You for a husband won't long tarry.
6. Proper and gay will be the man
   That will thee wed, my pretty Nan.

—

Whether a Maid shall have him she Loves.

1. Be not too coy, he is your own,
   But through delay he may be gone.
2. He of your wishes does not know;
   He'd soon comply if it were so.
3. Come, set thy heart at rest, I say,
   He will but plunder, and away.
4. Fear not, thy neighbor is the man,
   And he will have thee if he can.
5. Show him mere kindness, he will speak—
   His heart with silence else will break.
6. Sigh thou no more; he does relent,
   And his inconstancy repent.

How many husbands you may expect, etc., etc.

1. Come, in the town thou first shalt wed,
   A stranger next shall grace thy bed.
2. With one well loved, thy life shall be,
   And happy days, in marriage free.
3. The stars three husbands do presage,
   And thou shalt die in good old age.
4. Wed betimes, or else I fear
   Thou wilt not much for wedlock care.
5. Too much pride will make thee tarry,
   Yet, after all that, thou shalt marry.
6. Accept the ring thy love doth give;
   For long in wedlock he'll not live.

—

Whether it is best to Marry or not.

1. Don't fear, thy husband will be kind,
   And it is one shall please thy mind.
2. If he be of complexion fair,
   For thee that man I do prepare.
3. Come, never fear, it will be well,
   Or say, I can no fortune tell.
4. Pray lose no time, for, if you do,
   Age will come on, and you will rue.
5. If this match slips, you may long stay;
   Then take kind Will without delay.
6. Cupid commands thee now to do 't,
   Then, prithee, make no more dispute.

—

Queries about Fortunate Days.

1. Each Monday in the year indifferent are,
   Yet the event thereof bids you beware.
2. On Tuesday cruel Mars doth reign;
   Beware of strife, lest blows you gain.
3. On Wednesday witty projects make,
   For Mercury the rule does take.
4. Mild Jove rules Thursday, do not fear,
   'Tis prosperous throughout the year.
5. Fair Venus Friday does approve,
   And on that day does prosper love.
6. Saturn next does rule, beware.
   And take in hand no great affair.
   Lastly, Sol rules, whose golden aspect shows
   He all things mildly does to good dispose.

Charms, Spells,
—and—
INCANTATIONS.

—

TO BE RESORTED TO AT CERTAIN SEASONS OF THE YEAR,
TO PROCURE BY DREAMS AN INSIGHT INTO FUTURITY,
PARTICULARLY IN REGARD TO THE ARTICLE OF MARRIAGE.

—

ST. AGNES' DAY.

Falls on the 21st of January; you must prepare yourself by a twenty-four hours' fast, touching nothing but pure spring water, beginning at midnight on the 20th to the same again on the 21st; then go to bed, and mind you sleep by yourself; and do not mention what you are trying to any one, or it will break the spell; go to rest on your left side, and repeat these lines three times:

St. Agnes be a friend to me

In the gift I ask of thee;

Let me this night my husband see—

and you will dream of your future spouse. If you see more men than one in your dream, you will wed two or three times, but, if you sleep and dream not, you will never marry.

—

ST. MAGDALEN.

Let three young women assemble together on the eve of this saint [July 22] in an upper apartment, where they are sure not to be disturbed, and let no one try whose age is more than twenty-one, or it breaks the charm; get rum, wine, gin, vinegar, and water, and let each have a hand in preparing the potion. Put it in a ground-glass vessel; no other will do. Then let each young woman dip a sprig of rosemary in, and fasten it in her bosom, and, taking three sips of the mixture, get into bed; and the three must sleep together, but not a word must be spoken after the ceremony begins, and you will have true dreams, and of such a nature that you cannot possibly mistake your future destiny. It is not particular as to the hour in which you retire to rest.

———

STRANGE BED.

Lay under your pillow a prayer-book, opened at the Matrimonial Service, bound round with the garters you wore that day and a sprig of myrtle, on the page that says, *with this ring I thee wed,* and your dream will be ominous, and you will have your fortune as well told as if you had paid a crown to an astrologer.

———

A SPELL.
(To be used at any convenient time.)

Make a nosegay of various colored flowers, one of a sort, a sprig of rue, and some yarrow off a grave, and bind all together with the hair from your head; sprinkle them with a few drops of the oil of amber, using your left hand, and bind the flowers round your head under your night-cap when you retire to rest; put on clean sheets and linen, and your future fate will appear in your dream.

———

PROMISES OF MARRIAGE.

If you receive a written one, or any declaration to that effect in a letter, prick the words with a sharp-pointed needle on a sheet of paper quite clear from any writing; fold in nine folds, and place it under your head when you retire to rest. If you dream of diamonds, castles, or even a clear sky, there is no deceit and you will prosper. Trees in blossom, or flowers, show children; washing, or graves, show you will lose them by death; and water shows they are faithful, but that you will go through severe poverty with the party for some time, though all may end well.

———

TO KNOW YOUR HUSBAND'S TRADE.

Exactly at twelve, on Midsummer-day [summer solstice], place a bowl of water in the sun, pour in some boiling pewter as the clock is striking, saying thus:
Here I try a potent spell,
Queen of love and Juno tell,
In kind love to me,
What my husband is to be;
This the day, and this the hour,
When it seems you have the power
For to be a maiden's friend.
So, good ladies, condescend.

A tobacco-pipe full is enough. When the pewter is cold, take it out of the water, and drain it dry in a cloth, and you will find the emblems of your future husband's trade quite plain. If more than one, you will marry twice; if confused and no emblems, you will never marry; a coach shows a gentleman for you.

—

A CHRISTMAS SPELL.

Steep mistletoe berries, to the number of nine, in a mixture of ale, wine, vinegar, and honey; take them on going to bed, and you will dream of your future lot; a storm in this dream is very bad; it is most likely that you will marry a sailor, who will suffer shipwreck at sea; but to see either sun, moon, or stars is an excellent presage; so are flowers; but a coffin is an index of a disappointment in love.

THE NINE KEYS.

Get nine small keys; they must all be your own by begging or purchase (borrowing will not do, nor must you tell what you want them for); plait a three-plaited band of your own hair, and tie them together, fastening the ends with nine knots; fasten them with one of your garters to your left wrist on going to bed, and bind the other garter round your head; then say:

St. Peter take it not amiss,
To try your favor I've done this;
You are the ruler of the keys,
Favor me, then, if you please;

Let me then your influence prove,
And see my dear and wedded love.

This must be done on the eve of St. Peter's [June 29]. It is an old charm used by the maidens of Rome in ancient times, who put great faith in it.

———

THE THREE KEYS.

Purchase three small keys, each at a different place, and, on going to bed, tie them together with your garter, and place them in your left hand glove, along with a small flat dough cake, on which you have pricked the first letters of your sweetheart's name; put them in your bosom when you retire to rest; if you are to have that young man, you will dream of him, but not else.

———

To Know if a Woman with Child will have a Girl or a Boy.

Write the proper names of the father and the mother, and the month she conceived with child; count the letters in these words, and divide the amount by seven; and then, if the remainder be even, it will be a girl; if uneven, it will be a boy.

———

To Know if a Child New-Born Shall Iiive or Not.

Write the proper names of the father and mother, and of the day the child was born; count the letters in these words, and to the amount add twenty-five, and then divide the whole by seven; if the remainder be even, the child shall die, but if it be uneven, the child shall live.

—

To Know How Soon a Person will be Married.

Get a green pea-pod, in which are exactly nine peas; hang it over the door, and then take notice of the next person who comes in, who is not of the family, nor of the same sex with yourself, and if it proves an unmarried individual, you will certainly be married within that year.

—

A CHARM.

(To be used on the eve of any fast directed in the calendar.)

This takes a week's preparation, for you must abstain from meat or strong drink. Go not to bed till the clock has struck the midnight hour, and rise before seven the next morning, the whole seven days. You must neither play at cards, or any game of chance, nor enter a place of public diversion. When you go to bed on the night of trial, eat something very salty, and do not drink after it, and you may depend on having very singular dreams; and, being very thirsty, you will probably dream of liquids. Wine is excellent, and shows wealth or promotion; brandy, foreign lands; rum, that you will wed a sailor, or one that gets his living at sea; gin, but a middling life; cordials, variety of fortune; and water, if you drink it, poverty; but to see a clear stream is good. Children are not good to behold in this dream, nor cards, nor dice; they forebode the loss of reputation, or that you will never marry.

———

VALENTINE.

If you receive one of these love tokens, and cannot guess at the party who sent it, or are in any doubt, the following method will explain it to a certainty. Prick the fourth finger on your left hand, and, with a crow quill, write on the back of the valentine the day and hour on which you were born, and the date of the year, also of the present one, the moon's age, and the name of the present morning-star, all of which you will find in the almanac, and the sign into which the sun has entered. Try this on the first Friday after you receive the valentine, but do not go to bed till midnight; place the paper in your left shoe, and put it under your pillow; lay on your left side, and repeat three times:

St. Valentine, pray condescend
To be this night a maiden's friend;
Let me now my lover see,
Be he of high or low degree;
By a sign his station show,
Be it weal or be it woe;
Let him come to my bedside,
And my fortune thus decide.

The young woman will be sure to dream of the identical person who sent the valentine, aud may guess, by the other particulars of the dream, if or not he is to be her spouse.

———

YARROW.

This is a weed commonly found in abundance on graves towards the close of the spring and beginning of the summer. It must be plucked exactly on the first hour of morn; place three sprigs either in your shoe or glove, saying:

Good morning, good morning, good yarrow,
And thrice a good morning to thee;
Tell me before this time to-morrow
Who my true love is to be.

Observe, a young man must pluck the weed off a young maiden's grave, and a female must select that of a bachelor's; retire home to bed without speaking a word, or it dissolves the spell; put the yarrow under your pillow, and it will procure a sure dream, on which you may depend.

To Know whether a Woman shall have the Man She Wishes.

Get two lemon peels and wear them all day, one in each pocket, and at night rub the four posts of the bedstead with them; if she is to succeed, the person will appear in her sleep, and present her with a couple of lemons; if not, there is no hope.

To Know if any one shall Enjoy their Love or not.

Take the number of the first letter of your name, the number of the planet, and the day of the week; put all these together, and divide them by thirty; if it be above, it will come to your mind, and if below, to the contrary; and mind that number which exceeds not thirty.

SIGNS TO CHOOSE

GOOD HUSBANDS AND WIVES.

—

1. If the party be of a ruddy complexion, high and full-nosed, his eyebrows bending archwise, his eyes standing full, of a black and lively color, it denotes him good-natured, ingenious, and born to good fortune, and the like in a woman, if born under the planet Jupiter.

2. If the party be phlegmatic, lean, and of a dusky complexion, given much to musing and melancholy, beware of such a one, of what sex soever.

3. An indifferent wide mouth, and full cheeks, smooth forehead, little ears, dark-brown hair, and a chin proportionate to the face, is very promising.

4. An extraordinarily long chin, with the underlip larger than the upper, signifies a cross-grained person, fit for little business, yet given to folly.

5. A well-set, broad chin in a man, his face being round, and not too great, and a dimple or dent in a woman's cheek or chin, denotes they will come together and live happily.

PREDICTIONS CONCERNING

Children Born on any Day in the Week.

—

SUNDAY.—The child born on Sunday will obtain great riches, be long-lived, and enjoy much happiness.

MONDAY.—Children born on this day will not be very successful in most enterprises they may engage in, being irresolute, subject to be imposed upon through their good-natured disposition; they are generally willing and ready to oblige every one who asks a favor from them.

TUESDAY.—The person born on this day will be subject to violent starts of passion, and not easily reconciled; if a man, given to illicit connections, from which conduct many serious consequences and misfortunes will arise, and he will never be safe, being in danger of suffering death by violence, if he does not put a restraint upon his vicious inclinations.

WEDNESDAY.—The child ushered into the world on this day will be of a studious and sedate turn of mind; and if circumstances will allow, fond of perusing the literary works of the most talented ancient and modern authors. Should facilities be afforded to such a one, there is every probability of his being a highly-gifted author.

THURSDAY.—Those who first see the light on this day may in general have applied to them the appellation of being "born with a silver spoon in their mouths"; for, unless they resolutely spurn from them the Plutonic deity, riches will be poured into their lap with no niggard hand.

FRIDAY.—The little stranger who first inhales the vital air on this day will be blessed with a strong constitution, and will be lucky in every enterprise through life, happy in his or her domestic relations, and finally die rich and lamented.

SATURDAY.—This is an unlucky day for being ushered into this world of sin and sorrow; but those born on this last day of the week may become good members of society, honored and respected by their fellow-creatures, and blessed by the Almighty.

To Discover a Thief by the Sieve and Shears.

Stick the points of the shears in the wood of the sieve, and let two persons support it, balanced upright, with their two fingers; then read a certain chapter in the Bible, and afterwards ask St. Peter and St. Paul if A or B is the thief, naming all the persons you suspect. On naming the real thief, the sieve will suddenly turn round about.

A NEW METHOD OF

Telling Fortunes by Cards.

Take out of the pack all the cards under seven, only reverse the aces, as these are called the points, and are of most particular consequence; then take out the eights, for they are cards of no meaning; you will then have twenty-eight left, which you must manage; shuffle them well, and deal them into four equal parcels; having first decided of what suit you will be the queen, and you must make your lover, or husband, of the same suit as yourself without regard to his complexion; take up the parcel dealt exactly before you, and then proceed regularly round to the right, examining them separately as you proceed. The first tells what is to happen soon, the second at some distance, and the third respects your husband or lover, and the fourth your secret wishes, and you must judge by the cards as to your success.

Signs of a Speedy Marriage, and good
success attending it, by
sundry signs.

1. For a woman to have the first and last letters of her Christian name the same with the man's surname that makes love to her denotes a great union and a generous love.

2. For a man to have the first and last letters of his Christian name the same with the woman's surname denotes the same.

3. To think on a party on a sudden awakening, without any meditation, on a Friday morning that before had a place in the affection of a man or woman is a demonstration of love or extraordinary friendship.

4. If a ring falls accidentally off a man's finger that is under no obligation of marriage and runs directly to the feet of a maid or widow, it denotes that he is not only in love with the widow, but that a sudden marriage will ensue.

5. The singing of a robin red-breast at your window, in the time of courtship, on a Wednesday, is a sign that you shall have the party desired.

6. If, when walking abroad with your sweetheart, you perceive a pair of pigeons circle you round, it is a sign of marriage and happiness to ensue, with much content.

7. If a hare cross you on Saturday morning, it promises happy days, riches, and pleasure.

THE WEATHER.

In the evening when the horizon in the West is tinged with a ruddy glow, it is a sign that bright and dry weather will speedily follow.

When the sky appears ruddy in the East In the evening, changeable weather may be confidently anticipated.

Should the horizon in the North wear a ruddy appearance in the evening, stormy and boisterous weather may be expected.

If the clouds in the South are ruddy la the evening, sunshiny and rainy weather will prevail for some time afterwords.

When the rays from the sun at mid-day are more than ordinarily dazzling, rainy weather will shortly succeed.

In summer-time, when the swallows fly near to the ground, rainy weather will assuredly soon follow.

The shrill crowing of the cock during rainy weather is a sign that a drought will speedily prevail.

When the smoke from the chimney falls down towards the ground, instead of rising upwards, it is a sign that rainy weather will soon follow.

When the face of the moon is partially obscured by a light thing vapor, rain will shortly follow.

If on a foggy morning in summer the fog rises upwards, it will be a fine day; if the fog falls to the ground, it will be wet.

When you see the fowls in a farm-yard flocking together under some covert, be assured that ungenial weather is about to succeed.

When the rooks, on flying over your head, make an extraordinary and discordant cawing, rain will come on shortly.

When you see your dog or cat more than ordinarily restless, frisking about the house in all directions, be assured that some boisterous weather will shortly succeed.

In rainy weather, when you hear the chirping of the sparrows on the house-top more shrill than usual, it is a sign that clear and dry weather will quickly succeed.

When you see a vapory fluid resting upon a stagnant pond on the fore-part of the day, you may conclude that rainy weather will shortly come on. Should the vapor ascend and clear away, a continued drought may be anticipated.

In summer, when the atmosphere is dense and heavy, and there is scarcely a breath of air, be assured that thunderstorm is coming on.

When the firmament is lighted up with meteoric phenomens, such as falling stars, globes of fire, etc., changeable and boisterous weather may be expected to prevail.

When the rising sun appears like a solid mass of fervent-heated metal, and no rays appear to emanate therefrom, fine and dry weather may be confidently anticipated.

When the sun sets in a halo of ruddy brightness, genial and bright weather may be fully relied on for the coming day.

When the moon appears of a ruddy hue, stormy and boisterous weather may be expected to follow.

When the stars appear of a sparkling brightness, fine and genial weather may be expected to prevail fro some time. Should the stars appear obscure and dim, changeable and rainy weather may be anticipated.

When in summer-time, you see the cattle grazing in a field gathering together in groups, be assured that a thunderstorm is approaching.

The luminous appearance of the Aurora Borealis, or Northern Lights, in the firmament foretells the approach of stormy and boisterous weather.

When the setting sun in Autumn or Winter seasons appears ruddy, it is a sign that high and boisterous winds may be expected to blow from the North and Northwest. When the sun at its rising in the Autumn or Winter seasons appears ruddy, it foretells that high and boisterous winds may be anticipated to blow from the South and Southeast.

When the sea-birds are observed flocking towards the shore, storms and tempests may be confidently expected.

When in the Autumn season, the migratory birds are seen flocking together, and taking their departure, it is a certain sign that rough and boisterous weather is approaching, and that a severe winter may be anticipated.

When the doves around a dove-cote make a more than ordinary cooing, and frequently pass in and out of their cote, it is a sign that a change of weather is near.

When the robin approaches your habitation, it is a sign that wintry weather will shortly prevail.

When there is a thick and vapory mist resting on the tops of the hills high in the morning, and remains there during the day, it is a sign that wet and ungenial weather may be anticipated. Should the mist eventually rise upward, and be evaporated by the sun's rays, a return to fine, dry weather may be looked for; if, however, the mist falls down into the valley, a continuation of wet weather will prevail.

Signs and Omens.

Auguries and Forewarnings.

However sceptical some persons may profess to be on the subject of signs, auguries, and forewarnings, still few will venture to deny that in innumerable instances those mysterious admonitions and forewarnings have been speedily followed by events of a pleasant or a painful nature to those who have received them. The belief in signs and auguries has been cherished by mankind ever since the creation; and this faculty is not confined to the human family alone, but the lower animals possess it, some of them in an extraordinary degree. The following are a few of the multifarious signs and auguries which admonish and forewarn mankind, at one time or another:

Should you be the subject of a deep depression of spirits, contrary to your usual constitutional buoyancy and liveliness, it is a sign that you are about to receive some agreeable intelligence.

If the crown of your head itches more than ordinary, you may expect to be advanced to a more honorable position in life.

Should the hair on your head come off, when combing, in greater quantities than usual, it is a sign that you will soon be the subject of a severe attack of affliction.

If your right eye-brow should immoderately itch, be assured that you are going to look upon a pleasant sight—a long-absent friend, or a long-estranged, but now reconciled, lover.

Should your left eye-brow be visited with a tantalizing itching, it is a sign that you will soon look upon a painful sight—the corpse of a valued friend, or your lover walking with a favored rival.

A ringing in your right ear is an augury that you will shortly hear some pleasant news.

A ringing in your left ear is a sign that you will in a short time receive intelligence of a very unpleasant nature.

When your left ear tingles some one is backbiting you.

A violent itching of the nose foretells trouble and sorrow to those who experience it.

An itching of the lips is a sign that some one is speaking disrespectfully of you.

When you are affected by an itching on the back of your neck, be assured that either yourself or some one nearly related to you is about to suffer a violent death.

An itching on the right shoulder signifies that you will shortly have a large legacy bequeathed to you.

When you feel an itching sensation on your left shoulder, be sure that you are about to bear a heavy burden of sorrow and trouble.

If your right elbow joint itches, you may expect shortly to hear some intelligence that will give you extreme pleasure.

Should you be annoyed with a violent itching on your left elbow joint, you may be sure that some vexatious disappointment will be experienced by you.

If you feel an itching on the palm of your right hand, you may expect soon to receive some money which you have been long expecting.

When the palm of your left hand itches, you may expect to be called upon to pay some money for a debt which you have not personally incurred.

An itching on the spine of your back is a sign that you will shortly be called upon to bear a heavy burden of sorrow and trouble.

An itching on your loins is an indication that you will soon receive an addition to your family, if married; if single, that you are on the eve of marriage.

When you are affected with an itching on the belly, expect to be invited to feast upon a choice collection of savory meats.

When either or both of your thighs itch, be assured that you are about to change your sleeping apartment.

If you have an itching sensation in your right knee, depend upon it that you will shortly undergo a remarkable and beneficial change in your previous course of life, and become religiously inclined.

If a similar sensation prevails in your right knee, you may expect to undergo a change in your deportment of an unfavorable nature.

An itching sensation on the shins foretells that you will be visited with a painful and long-continued affliction.

When your ankle-joints itch, be sure that you are about to be united to one whom you love, if single; if married, that your domestic comforts will be largely increased.

When the sole of your right foot itches, you may feel assured that you are about to undertake a journey from which you will derive much pleasure and enjoyment.

Should you experience a similar sensation on the sole of your left foot, you may expect to be called upon to take a journey of an unpleasant and melancholy nature.

If, in taking a walk, you should see a single magpie, it is a bad omen, especially if it should fly past you to the left hand; but if it should pass you to the right hand, the good will counterbalance the bad. Should you see two magpies together, expect to hear of something to your advantage—a proposal of marriage, if single; or a legacy of money bequeathed to you. Should the magpies fly past you together to your right hand, your own marriage, or the marriage of some one nearly related to you, will occur in a short time. The seeing of several magpies together is considered a very fortunate omen.

May is considered an unlucky month to marry in, therefore avoid doing so if possible. If you can catch a snail by the horns on the first of May, and throw it over your shoulders, you will be lucky throughout the year. If you place one on a slate on that day, it will describe by its turnings the initials of your future partner's name.

If a young man or young woman, on going up a flight of stairs, should stumble in the middle of the flight, it is a sign that his or her marriage will take place in a short time. If the stumbling should be near the top of the stairs, then his or her marriage will be immediately consummated.

If a young person, when seated at the tea-table, should observe one or more stalks of the tea-plant in the newly-poured-out cup, and if, on stirring the tea and holding the spoon in the middle of the liquid, the stalk or stalks should come close to the spoon-handle, it is a token that he or she will be soon married.

When the house-dog is unusually restless, and howls dismally in the night-time, it is a sign that sickness and death are about to visit the family to whom the dog belongs.

When the wick of your candle shows a bright spark in the midst of the flame, it is a sign that a long-absent friend is about to visit you.

When the ribs of your fire-grate are more than usually covered with flakes of soot, it is a sign that a stranger is about to visit your habitation.

—

The *Bannich Brauder*, or "dreaming bannocks," are very much thought of by the Scotch. They contain "a little of that substance which chimney-sweeps call soot." In baking them "the baker must be as mute as a stone— one word would destroy the whole concern." Each person has one, slips off quietly to bed, lays his or her head on the bannock, and the sweetheart of each appears in dreams during sleep.

The Moon.

—

1. A child born within twenty-four hours after the new moon will be fortunate and live to a good old age. Whatever is dreamt on that day will be fortunate and pleasing to the dreamer.

2. The second day is very lucky for discovering things lost, or hidden treasure; the child born on this day shall thrive.

3. The child born on the third day will be fortunate through persons in power, and whatever is dreamed will prove true.

4. The fourth day is bad; persons falling sick on this day rarely recover.

5. The fifth day is favorable to begin a good work, and the dreams will be tolerably successful; the child born on this day will be vain and deceitful.

6. The sixth day the dreams will not immediately come to pass, and the child born will not live long.

7. On the seventh day do not tell your dreams, for much depends on concealing them; if sickness befalls you on this day, you will soon recover; the child born will live long, but have many troubles.

8. On the eighth day the dreams will come to pass; whatever business a person undertakes on this day will prosper.

9. The ninth day differs very little from the former; the child born on this day will arrive at great riches and honor.

10. The tenth day is likely to be fatal; those who fall sick will rarely recover, but the child born on this day will live long and be a great traveller.

11. The child that is born on the eleventh day will be much devoted to religion, of an engaging form and manners.

12. On the twelfth day the dreams are rather fortunate, and the child born shall live long.

13. On the thirteenth day the dreams will prove true in a very short time.

14. If you ask a favor of any one on the fourteenth day, it will be granted.

15. The sickness that befalls a person on the fifteenth day is likely to prove mortal.

16. The child that is born on the sixteenth day will be of very ill-manners and unfortunate; it is nevertheless a good day for the buying and selling of all kinds of merchandise.

17. The child born on the seventeenth day will be very foolish; it is a very unfortunate day to transact any kind of business, or contract marriage.

18. The child born on the eighteenth day will be valiant, but will suffer considerable hardships; if a female, she will be chaste and industrious, and live respected to a great age.

19. The nineteenth day is dangerous; the child born will be very ill-disposed and malicious.

20. On the twentieth day the dreams are true, but the child born will be dishonest.

21. The child born on the twenty-first day will grow up healthy and strong, but be of a very selfish, ungenteel turn of mind.

22. The child born on the twenty-second day will be fortunate; he or she will be of a cheerful countenance, religious, and much beloved.

23. The child that is born on the twenty-third day will be of an ungovernable temper, will forsake his friends, and choose to wander about in a foreign country, and will be very unhappy through life.

24. The child born on the twenty-fourth day will achieve many heroic actions, and will be much admired for his extraordinary abilities.

25. The child born on the twenty-fifth day will be very wicked; he will meet with many dangers, and is likely to come to an ill end.

26. On the twenty-sixth day the dreams are certain; the child then born will be rich, and much esteemed.

27. The twenty-seventh day is very favorable for dreams, and the child then born will be of a sweet and amiable disposition.

28. The child born the twenty-eighth day will be the delight of his parents, but will not live to any great age.

29. Children born on the twenty-ninth day will experience many hardships, though in the end they may turn out happily. It is good to marry on this day; and business begun on this day will be prosperous.

30. The child that is born on the thirtieth day will be fortunate and happy, and well skilled in the arts and sciences.

THE MYSTERIOUS WATCH.

Request any person to lend you his watch, and ask him if it will go when laid on the table. He will, no doubt, answer in the affirmative; in which case, place the watch over the end of a concealed magnet, and it will presently stop. Then mark the precise spot where you placed the watch, and moving the point of the magnet, give the watch to another person, and desire him to make the experiment; in which he not succeeding, give it to a third (at the same time replacing the magnet), and he will immediately perform it to the great chagrin of the second party.

The experiment cannot be effected unless you take the precaution to use a very strongly impregnated magnetic bar, nor unless the balance-wheel of the watch be of steel, which may be ascertained by previously opening it and looking at the works.

PHYSIOLOGICAL SIGNS
—OF—

Character and Disposition.

———

STRENGTH OF BODY is known by a stiff hair, large bones, firm and erect, the head broad and high, the forehead short, hard, and peaked, with bristly hair, large feet, rather thick and broad, a harsh, unequal voice and choleric complexion.

WEAKNESS OF BODY is distinguished by a small, ill-proportioned head, narrow shoulders, soft skin, and melancholy complexion.

THE SIGNS OF LONG LIFE are strong teeth, a sanguine temperament, middle size, large, deep and ruddy lines in the hand, large muscles, stooping shoulders, full chest, firm flesh, clear complexion, slow growth, wide ears, and large eyelids.

SHORT LIFE may be inferred from a thick tongue, the appearance of grinders before age of puberty, thin, straggling, and uneven teeth, confused lines in the hand, of a quick but small growth.

A GOOD GENIUS may be expected from a thin skin, middle stature, blue bright eyes, fair complexion, straight and pretty strong hair, an affable aspect, the eyebrows joined, moderation in mirth, an open, cheerful countenance, and the temples a little concave.

A DUNCE may be known by a swollen neck, plump arms, sides and loins, a round head, concave behind, a large, fleshy forehead, pale eyes, a dull, heavy look, small joints, snuffling nostrils, and a proneness to laughter, little hands, an ill-proportioned head—either too big or too little—blubber lips, short fingers, and thick legs.

FORTITUDE is promised from a wide mouth, a sonorous voice, grave, slow, and always equal, upright posture, large eyes, pretty open; and steadfast, the hair high above the fore-head, the head much compressed or flattened, the forehead square and high, the extremities large and robust, the neck firm, though not fleshy; a large, corpulent chest, and brown complexion.

BOLDNESS is characterized by a prominent mouth, rugged appearance, rough forehead, arched eyebrows, large nostrils and teeth, short neck, great arms, ample chest, square shoulders, and a froward countenance.

PRUDENCE is generally distinguished by a head which is flat on the sides, a broad, square forehead, a little concave in the middle, a soft voice, a large chest, thin hair, light eyes—either blue, brown or black—large ears, and an equaline nose.

A GOOD MEMORY is commonly attached to those persons who are smaller, yet better formed in the upper than the lower parts, not fat but fleshy, of a fair, delicate skin, with the pole of the head uncovered, crooked nose, teeth thick set, large ears, with plenty of cartilage.

A BAD MEMORY is observable in persons who are larger in their superior than inferior parts, fleshy, though dry and bald.

A GOOD IMAGINATION AND THOUGHTFUL DISPOSITION is distinguished by a large, prominent forehead, a fixed and attentive look, slow respiration, and an inclination of the head.

A GOOD SIGHT is enjoyed by those persons who have generally black, thick, straight eye-lashes, large, bushy eyebrows, concave eyes, contracted, as it were, inwards.

SHORT-SIGHTED PEOPLE have a stern, earnest look, small, short eyebrows, large pupils, and prominent eyes.

SENSE OF HEARING—Those who possess the same in perfection have ears well furnished with gristle, well channelled and hairy.

THE SENSE OF SMELLING is most perfect in those who have large noses, descending very near the mouth, neither too moist nor too dry.

A NICE FACULTY OF TASTING is peculiar to such as have a spongy, porous, soft tongue, well moistened with saliva, yet not moist.

DELICACY IN THE TOUCH belong to those who have a soft skin, sensitive nerves, and nervous sinews, moderately warm and dry.

IRASCIBILITY is accompanied by au erect posture, a clear skin, a solemn voice, open nostrils, moist temples, displaying superficial veins, thick neck, equal use of both hands, quick pace, blood-shot eyes, large, unequal, ill-ranged teeth, and choleric disposition.

TIMOROUSNESS resides where we find a concave neck, pale color, weak, winking eyes, soft hair, smooth, plump breast, shrill, tremulous voice, small mouth, thin lips, broad, thin hands, and small shambling feet.

MELANCHOLY is denoted by a wrinkled countenance, dejected eyes, meeting eyebrows, slow pace, fixed look, and deliberate respiration.

AN AMOROUS DISPOSITION may be known by a fair, slender face, a redundancy of hair, rough temples, broad forehead, moist, shining eyes, wide nostrils, narrow shoulders, hairy hands and arms, well-shaped legs.

GAIETY attends a serene, open forehead; rosy, agreeable countenance; a sweet, musical tone of voice; an agile body, and soft flesh.

ENVY appears with a wrinkled forehead, frowning, dejected, and squinting look, a pale, melancholy countenance, and a dry, rough skin.

INTREPIDITY often resides in a small body, with red, curled hair; ruddy countenance, frowning eyebrows, arched and meeting, eyes blue or yellowish, large mouth, and red lines in the hand.

GENTLENESS OR COMPLACENCY may be distinguished by a soft and moist palm, frequency of shutting the eyes, soft movement, slow speech, soft, straight, and lightish-colored hair.

BASHFULNESS may be discovered by moist eyes, never wide open, eyebrows frequently lowered, blushing cheeks, moderate pace, slow and submissive speech, bent body, and glowing ears of a purple hue.

TEMPERANCE OR SOBRIETY is accompanied with equal respiration, a medium-sized mouth, smooth temples, eyes of an ordinary size, either fair or azure, and a short, flat body.

STRENGTH OF MIND is signified by light, curled hair; a small body, shining eyes, but a little depressed; a grave, intense voice, bushy beard, large, broad back and shoulders.

PRIDE stands confessed with large eyebrows, a large, prominent mouth, a broad chest, slow pace, erected head, shrugging shoulders, and staring eyes.

LUXURY dwells with a ruddy or pale complexion, downy temples, bald pate, little eyes, thick neck, corpulent body, large nose, thin eyebrows, and hands covered with a kind of down.

LOQUACITY may be expected from a bushy beard, broad fingers, pointed tongue, eyes of a ruddy hue, a large, prominent upper lip, and a sharp, pointed nose.

PERVERSENESS may be dreaded when we perceive a high forehead, firm, short, thick, immoveable neck, quick speech, immoderate laughter, fiery eyes, and short, fleshy hands and fingers.

PHYSIOGNOMICAL SIGNS OF A GOOD GENIUS.

A straight, erect body, neither over-tall or short, between fat and thin, the flesh naturally soft, the skin neither soft nor rough, but a medium between; the complexion white, verging to blush of redness; the hair between hard and soft, usually of a brown color; the head and face of a moderate size; the forehead rather high; the eyes manly, big, and clear, of a blue or hazel color; the aspect mild and humane; the teeth so mixed that some are broad and some are narrow; a subtle tongue, and the voice between intense and remiss; the neck comely and smooth; the channel-bone of the throat appearing and moving; the back and ribs not over-fleshy; the shoulders plain and slender; the hand indifferently long and smooth; the fingers long, smooth, and equally distant; the nails white, mixed with red, and shining; and the carriage of the body erect in walking.

SIGNS OF A CHOLERIC DISPOSITION

1. The habit of the body hot in touch, dry, lean, hard and hairy.

2. The color of the face yellow.

3. A natural dryness of the mouth and tongue.

4. The thirst great and frequent.

5. Activity and inquietude of the body.

6. The pulse hard, swift, and often beating.

7. The spittle bitter.

8. The dreams are mostly of yellow things—of brawls, of fights, and quarrels.

—

SIGNS OF A SANGUINE CONSTITUTION

1. The habit of the body hot in touch, fleshy, soft and hairy.

2. The color of the body fresh, sanguine, and lively.

3. A natural, constant blush in the face.

4. The pulse soft, moist and full.

5. The sweetness of the spittle.

6. Dreams, most commonly of red things—of beauty, feasting, dancing, music, and all jovial and pleasing recreations.

7. A continual habit of pleasantness and affability.

8. Often affected with jests, mirth and laughter.

—

SIGNS OF A PHLEGMATIC CONSTITUTION.

1. The habit of the body cold and moist; in touch, soft; fat, gross, and not hairy.

2. A constant natural whiteness or wanness in the face.

3. The pulse soft, slow and rare.

4. The thirst little, and seldom desiring drink.

5. The dreams usually are of white things—floods, inundations, and accidents belonging to water.

6. Sleep much and frequent.

7. Slowness and dullness of the body to exercise.

—

SIGNS OF A MELANCHOLY CONSTITUTION.

1. The body in touch cold, dry, lean and smooth.

2. The body of a dark, dull, gloomy, leaden color.

3. The spittle in little quantity and sour.

4. Pulse little, rare and hard.

5. The dreams often of black and terrible things—of spirits, ghosts, dreadful apprehensions, choking, and beheading; mad beasts, as oxen, wolves and tigers, ready to devour you.

6. Greatly oppressed with fear.

7. A stability in cogitations, and constancy in the performance of the thing intended.

Physiognomy

—

Of Physiognomy.

—

Of Prognostics to be Drawn from the Color and Nature of the Hair of Men and Women—As Also from the Forehead, Eyebrows, Eyes, Nose, Mouth, Chin, and Whole Assemblage of Features.

Astrology is a celestial science that treats of the doctrine of the stars, which are placed in the firmament of heaven for the use and benefit of man; and it is proved, by daily observation and experience, that the fate of every person in existence is not only written in the heavens at the time of each of their said births, but that the same is also stamped and marked out in the face and hands of every man. The one is called *Physiognomy*, and the other *Chiromancy*, or *Palmistry*—so that the fate of every person is written in three places, at the birth of every individual, viz.: first, in the heavens; secondly, in their faces; and thirdly, in their hands; and I shall therefore proceed to inform your judgment and understanding in the science of physiognomy. In the first place, observe the following rules;

1. The gentleman whose hair is very black and smooth, hanging far over his shoulders, and in large quantity, is mild but resolute; cool, until greatly provoked; not much inclined to excess of any kind, but

he may be persuaded to it. He is constant in his attachments, and not liable to many misfortunes.

2. A lady of the same kind of hair is moderate in her desires of every kind, addicted to reflection, and though not subject to violence in love, is steady in her attachments, and no enemy to its pleasures; of a constitution neither vigorous nor feeble.

3. If the hair is very black, short, and curling, the gentleman will be much given to liquor, somewhat quarrelsome, and of an unsettled temper; more amorous, and less steady in his undertakings, but ardent at the beginning of an enterprise. He will be desirous of riches, but will often be disappointed in his wishes therein.

4. The same may be said of a lady.

5. A gentleman with dark-brown, long, and smooth hair is generally of a robust constitution; obstinate in his temper, eager in his pursuits, a lover of the fair sex, fond of variety, in his ordinary pursuits exceedingly curious, and of a flexible disposition. He will live long, unless guilty of early intemperance.

6. A lady of the same kind of hair will be nearly the same as the gentleman, but more steady in her conduct and attachments, especially in love. She will be of a good constitution, have many children, enjoy good health, and a reasonable share of happiness.

7. If the hair is short and bushy, it will make very little alteration in the gentleman or lady, but that the gentleman will be more forward to strike when provoked, and the lady will be more of a scold.

8. A gentleman with light-brown, long, smooth hair is of a peaceable, even, and rather generous temper; will prevent mischief, if in his power, but when very much provoked, will strike furiously; but is afterwards sorry

for his passion, and soon appeased: strongly attached to the company of ladies, and will protect them from insult. Upon the whole, he is in general an amicable character, affable and kind.

9. A lady of the same kind of hair is tender-hearted, but hasty in temper; neither obstinate nor haughty; her inclination to love never unreasonable; her constitution will be good, but she will be seldom very fortunate.

10. A gentleman with fair hair will be of a weak constitution; his mind given much to reflection, especially in religious matters. He will be assiduous in his occupation, but not given to rambling; very moderate in amorous wishes, but not live to an old age.

11. A lady of this colored hair is on the contrary of a good constitution; never to be diverted from her purposes; passionate in love affairs, never easy unless in company, and delights in hearing herself praised, especially for beauty; delights in dancing and strong exercises, and commonly lives to a great age.

12. A gentleman with long, red hair is cunning, artful and deceitful; he is much addicted to traffic of some kind, restless in his disposition, constantly roving, and desirous of enjoying the pleasures of love. He is covetous of getting money, and spends it foolishly; he is indefatigable, and no obstacle will induce him to forsake his enterprise until he has seen the issue of it. He is inclined to timidity, but, by reflection, may correct it, and pass for a man of courage.

13. A lady of the same kind of hair is glib of tongue, talkative and vain; her temper is impatient and fiery, and will not submit to contradiction; she has a constant flow of spirits, and much given to the pleasures of love. However delicate her person may seem, her constitution

is generally vigorous; but she seldom lives to see old age, for obvious reasons; her promises are seldom to be depended upon, because the next object that engrosses her attention makes her forgetful of everything that preceded it, and will always resent any disappointment she may meet with.

I will now proceed to give some few instructions concerning the hair in other particulars, by the following remarks:

14. If the hair falls off at the forepart of the head, the person will be easily led, though otherwise rational, and will often be duped when he thinks he is acting right; he will likewise frequently meet with disappointments in money matters, which will either hurt his credit, or force him to shorten his expenses.

15. If the hair falls off behind, he will be obstinate, peevish, passionate, and fond of commanding others, though he has no right, and will grow angry if his advice is not followed. However preposterous, he will be fond of hearing and telling old stories and tales of ghosts and fairies, but will be a good domestic man, and provide for his family to the utmost of his power.

16. If the hair forms an arch round the forehead, without being much indented at the temples, both the gentleman and the lady will be innocent, credulous, moderate in all their desires, and though not ardent in their pursuits, will still be persevering. They will be modest, good-natured, prosperous and happy.

17. If the hair is indented at the temples, the person will be affable, steady, good-natured, prudent, and attentive to business, of a solid constitution, and long-lived.

18. If the hair descends low upon the forehead, the person will be selfish and designing; of a surly disposition, unsociable, and given to drinking. He will also be addicted to avarice, and his mind will be always intent upon the means of carrying on his schemes, etc.

19. The forehead that is large, round and smooth announces the lady or gentleman to be frank, open, generous and free, good-natured, and a safe companion; of a good understanding, and scorns to be guilty of any mean action; faithful to his promises, just in his dealings, steadfast in his engagements, and sincere in his affections; he will enjoy a moderate state of health, etc.

20. If the forehead is flat in the middle, the gentleman (or lady) will be found to be vain-glorious, and but little disposed to generosity; very tenacious of his honor, but brave; he will be fond of prying into the secrets of others, though not with the intention of betraying; them; he will be fond of reading newspapers, history, novels and plays; ardent, and very cautious of his own reputation.

21. If there be a hollow across the forehead, in the middle, with a ridge, as of flesh, above, and another below, the gentleman will be a good scholar, and the lady a great manufacturer, or attentive to whatever occupation she may be engaged in. They will be warm in argument or debate—they will be firm and steady in any point they fix their minds upon, and by their perseverance will generally carry their object; yet they will meet with many crosses, but will bear them with patience.

22. If the forehead juts out immediately at and over the eyebrows, running flat up to the hair, the gentleman or lady will be sullen, proud, insolent, imperious and

treacherous; they will be impatient when contradicted, apt to give great abuse, and to strike if they think they can do it with advantage. They will also impose upon any person, never forgiving any injury, and by their misconduct make themselves many enemies.

23. If the temples are hollow, with the bones advancing towards the forehead on either side, so that the space between must be necessarily flat, with a small channel or indenture rising from the upper part of the nose to the hair, the gentleman or lady will be of a daring and intrepid temper, introducing themselves into matters where they have no business, desirous of passing for wits, and of a subtle and enterprising nature; greedy of praise, quick in quarrel, and of a wandering disposition; very lewd, and full of resentment when they feel their pride hurt. In short, they delight in mischief, riots, etc.

24. If the eyebrows are very hairy, and that hair long and curled, with several of the hairs starting out, the gentleman or lady is of a gloomy disposition, litigious and quarrelsome, although a coward; greedy after the affairs of this world, perpetually brooding over some melancholy subject, and not an agreeable companion. He will be diffident, penurious, and weak in his understanding; never addicted to any kind of learning. He will pretend much friendship, but will make his affected passion subservient to his pecuniary designs, and also given to drinking, etc., etc.

25. If a gentleman or lady has long eyebrows, with some long hairs, they will be of a fickle disposition, weak-minded, credulous and vain, always seeking after novelties, and neglecting their own business; they will be talkative, pert and disagreeable in company; very

fond of contradition, but will not bear disappointment patiently; and also will be much addicted to drinking, etc.

26. If the eyebrows are thick and even—that is, without any or few starting hairs—the gentleman or lady will be of an agreeable temper, sound understanding and tolerable wit; moderately addicted to pleasure, fearful of giving offence; but intrepid and persevering in support of right; charitable and generous, sincere in their professions of love and friendship, and enjoy a good constitution.

27. If the eyebrow is small, thin of hair, and even, the gentleman and lady will be weak-minded, timorous, superficial, and not to be depended on; they will be desirous of knowledge, but will not have patience and assiduity enough to give it the necessary attention; but they will be desirous of praise for worthy actions, but will not have the spirit or perseverance enough to perform them in that degree of excellence that is requisite to attract the notice of wise men. They will be of a delicate constitution, etc.

28. If the eyebrow is thick of hair towards the nose, and goes off suddenly very thin, ending in a point, the gentleman or lady will be surly, capricious, jealous, fretful and easily provoked to rage; in their love they will be intemperate.

29. The eye that is large, full, prominent, and clear denotes a gentleman or lady to be of an ingenuous and candid disposition, void of deceit, and of an even, agreeable and affable disposition; modest and bashful in love, though by no means an enemy to its gratification; firm, though not obstinate; of a good understanding, of an agreeable but not brilliant wit; but clear and just in

argument, inclined to extravagance, and easily imposed upon.

30. The eye that is small but advanced in the head shows the gentleman or lady to be of a quick wit, sound constitution, lively genius, agreeable company and conversation, good morals, but rather inclined to jealously: attentive to business, fond of frequently changing his place, punctual in fulfilling his engagements, warm in love, prosperous in his undertakings, and generally fortunate in most things.

31. The gentleman or lady whose eyes are sunk in the head is of a jealous, distrustful, malicious, and envious nature; deceitful in their words and actions, never to be depended upon; cunning in over-reaching others, vainglorious, and associates with lewd and bad company, etc.

32. The gentleman or lady who squints, or have their eyes turned away, will be of a penurious disposition, but punctual in their dealings.

33. A black eye is lively, brisk, and penetrating, and proves the person who possesses it to be of a sprightly wit, lively conversation, not easily imposed upon, of a sound understanding, but, if taken on the weak side, may be led astray for a while.

34. A hazel eye shows the person to be of a subtle, piercing, and frolicsome turn, rather inclined to be arch, and sometimes mischievous, but good-natured at the bottom. He will be strongly inclined to love, and not over delicate in the means of gratifying that propensity.

35. A blue eye shows the person to be of a meek and gentle temper, affable and good-natured, credulous, and incapable of violent attachments; ever modest, cool, and undisturbed by turbulent passions; of a strong memory;

in constitution, neither robust nor delicate, subject to no violent impression from the vicissitudes of life, whether good or bad.

36. A gray eye denotes the person to be of a weak intellect, devoid of wit, but a plain, plodding, downright drudge, that will act as he is spirited up by others. He will be slow in learning anything that requires attention; he, however, will be just to the best of his understanding.

37. A wall eye denotes the person to be of a hasty, passionate, and ungovernable temper, subject to sudden and violent anger; haughty to equals and superiors, but mild and affable to his inferiors.

38. A red, or as it is vulgarly called, a saucer-eye, denotes the person to be selfish, deceitful, and proud, and furious in anger, fertile in the invention of plots, and indefatigable in his resolution to bring them to bear.

39. A nose that comes even on the ridge, flat on the sides, with little or no hollow between the eyes, declares the man to be sulky, insolent, disdainful, treacherous, and self-sufficient; if it has a point descending over the nostrils, he is avaricious and unfeeling, vain-glorious and ignorant; peevish, jealous, quick in resentment, yet a coward at the bottom.

40. A nose that rises with a sudden bulge a little below the eyes, and then falls again into a kind of hollow below, is petulant and noisy, void of science, and of a very light understanding.

41. The nose that is small, slender and peaked shows the person to be of a fearful disposition, jealous, fretful, and insidious, ever suspicious of those about him, catching at every word that he can interpret to his own advantage to ground his dispute upon, and also very curious to know what is said and done.

42. The nose that is small, tapering round in the nostrils, and cocked up, shows the person to be ingenuous, smart, of a quick apprehension, giddy, and seldom looking into consequences; but generous, agreeable, so as to carefully avoid giving offence; but resolute in doing himself justice when he receives an injury.

43. The lips that are thick, soft and long announces the person to be of a weak intellect, credulous, and slightly peevish; but by a little soothing easily brought back to a good humor. He is much addicted to the pleasures of love, and scarcely moderate in his enjoyment of them; yet he is upright in his conduct, and of a timorous temper.

44. If the underlip is much thicker than the upper, and more prominent, the person is of a weak understanding, but artful, knavish, and given to chicanery to the full extent of his ability.

45. The lips that are moderately plump and even declare the person to be good-humored, humane, sensible, judicious, and just; neither giddy nor torpid, but pursuing in every particular a just medium.

46. The lips that are thin show the person to be of a quick and lively imagination, ardent in the pursuit of knowledge, indefatigable in labor, not too much attached to money, eager in the pursuit of love, more brave than otherwise, and tolerably happy in life.

47. The lips that are thin and sunk inwards denote the person to be of a subtle and persevering disposition, everlasting in hatred, and never sparing any pains to compass his revenge; in love or friendship much more moderate and uncertain.

48. The chin that is round, with a hollow between it and the lip, shows the person to be of a good-humored disposition, kind and honest; he is sincere in his friendship, and ardent in his love; his understanding is good, and his genius capacious. If he has a dimple, it makes him better.

49. The chin that comes down flat from the edge of the lip and ends in a kind of chisel-form shows the person to be silly, credulous, ill-tempered, and greedy of unmerited honors; captious, wavering, and unsteady; he will affect great modesty in the presence of others, though he will not scruple to do the vilest actions when he thinks himself secure from discovery.

50. The chin that is pointed upwards shows the person to be much given to contrivances. However fair he may speak to you, you can never depend on his friendship, as his purpose is only to make you subservient to his own designs. In love his generosity will be of the same stamp.

51. Of the face in general, I shall say that the person whose features are strong, coarse, and unpleasant to the eye is of a selfish, brutal, rough, and unsociable disposition; greedy of money, harsh in expressions, but will sometimes fawn with a bad grace to gain his ends.

52. The face that is plump, round, and ruddy denotes the person to be of an agreeable temper, a safe companion, hearty, and jovial, fond of company, of sound principles and a clear understanding, faithful in love, etc.

53. The face that is thin, smooth, and even, with well-proportioned features, shows the person to be of a good disposition, but penetrating and active; somewhat inclined to suspicion, yet of an agreeable conversation;

assiduous in the pursuits of love, and strongly addicted to the delights of love.

54. A face whose cheek-bones jut out with thin jaws is of a restless and thinking disposition; fretful, etc.

55. A face that is pale by nature denotes a timorous disposition, but greatly desirous of carnal pleasures.

56. A face that is unequally red, whether streaked or appearing in spots, shows the person to be weak both in mind and body, yielding easily to affliction and sickness.

57. A face blotched shows the person to be addicted to drinking and vice, and not even free from any vice, though they have frequently the art to conceal the inclination.

58. The head that is large and round shows that the person has a tolerable understanding, but not near so good as he imagines; however, upon the whole, he is rather harmless, and not so much given to vice.

59. The head that is small and round, or if the face comes tapering, shows the person of an acute, penetrating disposition, much given to bantering and humor, but of very great sensibility, etc.

60. The head that is flat on either side, and deep from the face to the back, shows the person to be of a good understanding, deep penetration, great memory, and of an even and agreeable temper, but of slow belief, and not easily imposed upon.

NATIVITY.

—

TO CAST YOUR NATIVITY.

Having ascertained the exact time of your birth, and the hour in which you entered this transitory life, procure a Moore's almanac of that year, which will direct you to the sign that then reigned, the name of the planets, and the state of the moon; particularly observe whether the sun was just entering the sign, whether it was near the end, or what was its particular progress; if at the beginning, your fate will be strongly tinctured with its properties, moderate at the meridian, and slightly if the sun is nearly going out of the sign.

Write down the day of the week; see whether it is a lucky day or not, the state of the moon, the nature of the planets, and the influence described next, and you will ascertain your future destiny with very little trouble.

JANUARY.

(Aquarius, or the Water Bearer.)

Gives a love of wandering and variety, seldom contented long in one place; soon affronted, and slow to forgive; fond of law, though they lose the day. They are unhappy. Mercury gives them slights in love. A full moon is the best, for a new moon only adds to their false fears; and Saturn gives them real trouble to content with.

—

FEBRUARY.

(Pisces, or the Fishes.)

Those born under the influence of this planet prosper best on the ocean, or at a distance from their native home. But those horn under this sign, and not ordained to travel, will experience at times more or less distress. Mars and Jupiter are the best planets, and if the day of the week on which they were born be a fortunate one, let them begin their fresh concerns on that day, write and answer letters, or seek for money due to them according to their rule, and they have more than a chance for prosperity. The female traveller will be very fortunate, and have a contempt for danger, yet neither her disposition nor manners will be masculine; she will make an excellent wife and mother, and, if left a widow with children, will strive for their interest with a father's care and prudence; nor will she wed a second time, unless Venus rules her destiny. Mars give her success; Jupiter, vigilance; a new moon, virtue; a full moon, some enemies; and Saturn, temptation; yet she will prosper.

MARCH.

(Aries, or the Ram.)

A very good sign to those born under it. To either sex denotes prosperity, fidelity, dutiful children, and many liberal friends, but hot-tempered; if Mercury is one of the planets, they will then be very amiable. Jupiter and Venus are also good planets to them, but Mars or Saturn causes a sad alteration to their general destiny, and gives a mixed life of pain and pleasure. Venus reigning alone as a morning star at the time of their birth, causes them many amours.

—

APRIL.

(Taurus, or the Bull.)

To be prosperous under this sign will require active industry and patience under misfortunes and perils; but Jupiter, Venus, or the new moon, will soften this destiny. The men will be bold and adventurous, fond of governing, and hard to please; they must be careful not to enter on any fresh concern while their sign has the ascendency, the end of April and the two first weeks in May.

—

MAY.

(Gemini, or the Twins.)

Very fortunate for females, particularly in the grand article of matrimony, though they will prosper well in other affairs; the full moon and Venus are good for them. They will be punctual and honest in their dealings, he much respected by their friends and neighbors, and have many children.

—

JUNE.

(Cancer, or the Crab.)

A prosperous but eventful sign to both sexes, but more particularly those of of fair complexion; they will be exalted in life; Jupiter and Venus are the best signs for them; but, the brunettes, though fortunate, will plague themselves and others with whims, jealousies, and ill-nature, and may be very particular about mere trifles. If Mars be their planet, they will enter into lawsuits; and if Saturn, let them beware of ungovernable passions.

———

JULY.

(Leo, or the Lion.)

Favorable to those born in poverty, but not to the rich; for this sign always shows a great change of circumstances about the meridian of our days, sooner or later, according to the sign in which you were born. If Jupiter be the planet, the person born poor will become rich by legacies, or will probably marry their master or mistress, or his or her son or daughter, according to their sex, and lead a happy life. This has often proved true.

———

AUGUST.

(Virgo, or the Virgin.)

A most important sign; the men brave, generous, candid, and honest; the females amiable and prosperous, if they do not mar their own fortune by love of flattery, to which they will be prone, or else advancement awaits them. Venus is not a good planet for them, and Saturn shows seduction; but, if neither of these three planets predominate at the time of their birth, they will marry early, have good children, and enjoy the most valuable blessings of life, and have many unexpected gains.

———

SEPTEMBER.

(Libra, or the Balance.)

A middle course of life is promised by this sign; a smooth, even, unrippled stream, free from storms or sudden changes; in fact, an enviable destiny. The persons now born will be just in their transactions, faithful in love and wedlock, and averse to litigation and law; not many children, but those healthy.

———

OCTOBER.

(Scorpio, or the Scorpion.)

To the man, promises a long, active, useful life, and an intelligent mind; prosperous and very careful of what he gains; a good husband, parent and master, and a sincere friend; a little gay in his youthful days, but not vicious. Jupiter and a full moon adds to the good of his destiny; Saturn or Mercury will detract from it; Venus inclines him to the fair sex. To the woman this sign shows indolence; and, if she is well off in the world, it will not be by her own merit or industry, for she will have to thank those to whom it is her good fortune to be nearly allied; but, if she has no shining qualities that are prominent, she will be free from evil propensities, and will never bring disgrace on herself, her husband, her family, or friends, unless Venus reigned at her birth;

then I fear for her; but no other planet will affect her destiny.

—

NOVEMBER.
(Sagittarius, or the Archer.)

Gives to both sexes an amorous disposition, and, if Venus or Mercury presides at their birth, they will love variety; but Jupiter and Mars are good for them; the new moon is excellent to the female, and full to the man. It is seldom that persons born in this sign marry, if the first-mentioned planets reign; or, if they do marry, it is late in life, or when the meridian of their days are over, and they are become wise enough to relinquish folly; they then become steady and prudent, and generally do well; they seldom have many children, but what they have will prosper, and have friends who will promote their interest.

—

DECEMBER.
(Capricorn, or the Goat.)

Shows you will work and toil, and others reap the benefit of your labor, unless marriage alters the destiny; but hard will be your fate if your spouse is of the same sign as yourself; but, if Jupiter be one of the planets at your birth, the end of your days will be more prosperous than the beginning, after experiencing many cares and obstructions. A woman may probably better her fate by a second marriage, especially if Venus be her planet.

Love Presents and Witching Spells.

—

Take three hairs from your head, roll them up in a small compact form, and anoint them with three drops of blood from the left-hand fourth finger, choosing this because the anatomists say a vein goes from that finger to the heart; wear this in your bosom (taking care that none knows the secret) for nine days and nights; then enclose the hair in the secret cavity of a ring or a brooch, and present it to your lover. While it is in his possession, it will have the effect of preserving his love, and leading his mind to dwell on you. A chain or plait of your own hair, mixed with that of a goat, and anointed with nine drops of the essence of ambergris, will have a similar effect. Flowers prepared with your own blood will have an effect on your lover's mind; but the impression will be very transient, and fade with the flowers. If your love should be fortunate, and you are married to the object of your wishes, never reveal to him the nature of the present you made him, or it may have the fatal effect of turning love into hate.

Happiness and Affluence

—

"There is a tide in the affairs of men which, taken at the flood, leads on to fortune."
He that by the plow would thrive,
Himself must either hold or drive.
For age and want save while you may,
No morning's sun lasts a whole day.
Get what you can, and what you get hold;
'Tis a stone that will turn all your lead to gold.
Therefore be ruled by me, I pray—
Save something for a rainy day.

Remember that time is money; for he that can earn ten shillings a day at his labor and goes abroad or sits idle at home one-half of that day, though he spend but sixpence during his diversion or idleness, he ought not to reckon that the only expense; he hath really wasted, or, rather, thrown away, five shillings besides.

Remember that credit is money. If a man let his money lay in my hands after it is due, because he has a good opinion of my credit, he gives me the interest, or so much as I can make of the money during that time. This amounts to a very considerable sum where a man hath large credit, and also makes good use of it.

Remember that money is of a prolific or multiplying nature. Money will produce money, and its offspring will produce more; and so five shillings turned is six;

being turned again is seven and three-pence; and so on, till it becomes a hundred pounds; and the more there is of it, the more it will produce on every turning, so that the profits rise quicker and quicker; and he who throws away a crown destroys all that it might have produced, even some scores of pounds.

Remember this proverb: that the good paymaster is lord of another man's purse; for he who is known to pay punctually and exactly to the time he promises, may, at any time, and on any occasion, raise all the money his friends can spare. This is sometimes of great use, next to industry and frugality. Nothing can contribute more to the raising of a man in the world than punctuality in all his dealings. Therefore, never keep borrowed money one single hour beyond the time promised, lest the disappointment should shut up your friend's purse forever, as the most trifling actions that affect a man's credit ought always to be avoided.

The sound of the hammer at five o'clock in the morning, or at nine at night, being heard by a creditor, makes him easy six months longer; but if he sees you at a gaming table, or hears your voice in a tavern when you should be at work, he sends for his money the very next day, and demands it before it is convenient for you to pay him.

Beware of thinking all your own that you possess, and of living accordingly. This is a mistake that many people of credit fall into; but, in order to prevent this, always keep an exact daily account of both your expenses, and also of your daily income and profits; for, if you will only just take the trouble at first to enumerate particulars, you will discover unto you how wonderfully small, trifling expenses mount up to a large sum; by which you will also discern what might have been, and also what may for the future be saved without causing any great inconvenience. In short, the way to obtain riches, if you desire it, is as plain as the way to market, which depends chiefly on two things, viz.: industry and frugality. And take care that you waste neither time nor money, but daily make the best use of both. If you take care of the hours and days, the weeks and months and years will also take care of themselves.

I have always found, by constant experience, that any business, being first well contrived, is more than half done—for a sleeping fox catches no poultry. There will be sleep enough in the grave; and, also, that lost time is but seldom found again, for that which we generally call time enough always proves little enough; for sloth makes things difficult, while industry makes them easy.

He that rises late must trot hard all day, and shall scarce overtake his business at night—for laziness travels so slow that poverty soon overtakes him. Drive your business, but let not that drive you; for early to bed and early to rise is the way to become healthy, wealthy, and wise. Industry need not want while he who lives on a vain hope will die fasting; for we find that there is nothing to be done or accomplished under the sun without labor.

He that hath a trade hath an estate, and he that hath a profession hath an office and profit with honor, but then the trade must be worked at, and the profession well followed, or they will not enable you to pay rent and taxes; for, at the working-man's house, hunger looks in, but dares not enter—for industry pays debts, while despair increases them.

Diligence is the mother of good luck. As Solomon saith: "The diligent hand maketh rich, while he that dealeth with a slack hand becometh poor;" for God gives all things to industry. *Then plough deep while sluggards sleep,* and you shall have plenty, while others have reason to complain of hard times. Therefore, keep working while it is called to-day, for you know not how much you may be hindered to-morrow; and never leave that business to be done to-morrow which you can do to-day; for, since you are not sure of a single hour, throw not that away. How many are there who live daily by their wits, and who often break for want of a stock in hand, while industry gives comfort, plenty and respect.

Keep your shop well and then your shop will keep you. For it sometimes happens that the eye of a master will do more work than both his hands, and more especially if his head be any reasonable length; for the want of care generally doth more damage than the want of knowledge. If you do not overlook your workmen, you may just as well leave them your purse open; for the trusting too much to the care of others has completely ruined many a man. Therefore, if you would be wealthy, think of being careful and saving; for

"Women, wine, game, and deceit
Make the wealth small and the wants great."

HOW TO MAKE THE DUMB-CAKE.

—

In order to make the dumb-cake with perfection, it is necessary strictly to observe the following instructions:

Let any number of young women take a handful of wheaten flour (and from the moment the hand touches the flour, not a word is to be spoken by any of them during the process) and place it on a sheet of white paper; then sprinkle it over with as much salt as can be held betwixt the finger and thumb; then one of the damsels must bestow as much of her own water as will make it into dough; which being done, each of the company must roll it up, and spread it thin and broad; and each person must, at some distance from each other, make the first letters of her Christian and surname with a large, new pin towards the end of the cake (if more Christian names than one, the first letter of each must be made). The cake must then be set before the fire, and each person must sit down in a chair, as far distant from the fire as the room will admit, not speaking a single word all this while.

This must be done soon after eleven at night, and between that and twelve each person must turn the cake once; and in a few minutes after twelve the husband of her who is to be the first married will appear to lay his hand on that part of the cake which is marked with her name.

MOLES.

—

**Time-honored predictions of a person's
disposition and future lot
by the aid of Moles.**

Though moles are, in their substance, nothing else than excrescences, or ebullitions, which proceed from the state of the blood whilst the foetus is confined in the womb, yet they are not given in vain, as they are generally characteristic of the disposition and temper of those that bear them; and it is also proved by daily experience that from the shape, situation, and circumstances they bear a strong analogy to the events which are to happen to a person in future life. But before I presume to give any directions to those who are to form the prognostic, who are desirous to be duly enabled to pronounce an infallible judgment, I shall, in the first place, teach you how to tell and duly inform any person whom you never saw in your life, even at a hundred or ten thousand miles distance, on what particular parts of the body they have any.

—

MARKS, SCARS, OR MOLES.

FROM THE FIGURE OF THE HEAVENS AT THE TIME OF THEIR BIRTH, WITHOUT ANY OTHER COMMUNICATION OR REFERENCE WHATEVER.

In the first place, you must observe what sign that is which is upon the cusp of the ascendent, and in that part of the native's body which that signs governs there will be a mole. For instance, if Aries be the sign ascending at birth, the mole will be on the head or face; if Taurus, on neck or throat; if Gemini, on the arms or shoulders; if Cancer, on the breast; and upon any other part of the body which the sign ascending shall govern. Observe next in which of the houses the lord of the ascendent is posited, and in that part of the body the sign governs which happens to fall upon the cusp of that house, the native will have another mole. Next observe the sign descending on the cusp of the sixth house, and in whatever part of the body that sign governs the native will find another mole; and upon that member also which is signified by the sign wherein the lord of the sixth house is posited will be found another. Observe also what sign the moon is posited in, and in that part of the body which is governed by it shall the native or querent find another mole. If the planet Saturn be the significator, the mole is either black or of a dark color. If Mars be the significator, and in a fiery sign, it then resembles a scar, cut, or dent in the flesh, but in any other sign it is a red mole. If Jupiter be the significator, the mole is of a purple or bluish cast. If the sun, it is of an olive or chestnut color. If Venus, it is yellow; if Mercury, of a pale lead color; if the Moon, it is whitish, or participates of the color of that planet which she happens to be in aspect. And if the planet which gives the mole be much impeded or afflicted, the mark or mole will then be larger or more visible to the eye of the beholder.

If the sign and planet which gives the mark or mole be masculine, it is then situated on the right side of the body; but, if feminine, on the left side. If the significator or planet which gives the mole be found above the horizon—that is, from the cusp of the ascendent to the cusp of the seventh, either in the twelfth, eleventh, tenth, ninth, eighth, or seventh house—the mark or mole will be on the forepart of the body; but if the significator be under the earth—that is, in either the first, second, third, fourth, fifth, or sixth house—it will be situated on the back or hinder part of the body. If only a few degrees of the sign ascend upon the horoscope, or descend on the sixth, or if the lord of the ascendant, lord of the sixth, or the moon, be posited in the beginning of any sign, the said mole or mark will be found upon the member those signs govern. If half the degrees of a sign ascend, or the significators are posited in the middle of any sign, the mole or mark will be in the middle of the member; but if the last degrees of a sign ascend, or the significators are in the latter degrees of a sign, the said mark or mole will then be situated on the lower part of the member such sign governs.

These observations are of excellent use, in order to know whether a question be logical, fit, and proper to be judged; for if the question be found thus radical, the time rightly taken, and the querent of sufficient age, this rule will never be found to fail.

—

1. I shall now proceed to give you herein the common prognostications by moles found in all the various parts of the body, according to the doctrine of the ancients. And first, it is essentially necessary to know the size of the mole, its color, whether it be perfectly round, oblong, or angular; because each of these will add to or diminish the force of the indication. The larger the mole, the greater the prosperity or adversity of the person; the smaller the mole, the less will be his good or evil fate. If the mole is round, it indicates good; if oblong, a moderate share of fortunate events; if angular, it gives a mixture of good and evil; the deeper the color, the more it announces favor or disgrace; the lighter, the less of either. If it is very hairy, much misfortune may be expected; if but few long hairs grow upon it, it denotes that your undertakings will be prosperous.

2. A mole that stands on the right side of the forehead or right temple signifies that the person will arrive to sudden wealth and honor, according to their birth and situation in life; which must always be attended to with due consideration.

3. A mole on the right eyebrow announces speedy marriage, and that the person to whom you will be married will possess many amiable qualities and a good fortune.

4. A mole on the left of either of those three places anounces unexpected disappointment in your most sanguine wishes.

5. A mole on the outside corner of either eye denotes the person to be of a steady, sober, and sedate disposition; but will be liable to a violent death.

6. A mole on either cheek signifies that the person never shall rise abbve mediocrity in point of fortune,

though, at the same time, he never will fall into real poverty.

7. A mole on the nose shows that the person will have good success in most of his or her undertakings.

8. A mole on the lip, either upper or lower, proves the person to be fond of delicate things, and much given to the pleasures of love, in which he or she will most commonly be successful.

9. A mole on the chin foreshows that the person will be attended with great prosperity, and be highly esteemed.

10. A mole on the side of the neck shows that the person will narrowly escape suffocation; but will afterwards rise to great consideration by an unexpected legacy or inheritance.

11. A mole on the throat denotes that the person shall become rich by marriage.

12. A mole on the right breast declares the person to be exposed to a sudden reverse from comfort to distress by unavoidable accidents. Most of his children will be girls.

13. A mole on the left breast signifies success in undertakings, and an amorous disposition. Most of his children will be boys,

14. A mole on the bosom portends mediocrity of health and fortune.

15. A mole under the left breast, over the heart, foreshows that a man will be of a warm disposition, unsettled in mind, fond of rambling, and light in his conduct, hi a lady it shows sincerity in love, quick conception, and easy travail in child-birth.

16. A mole on the right side, over any part of the ribs, denotes the person to be pusillanimous, and slow in

understanding anything that may be attended with difficulty.

17. A mole on the belly denotes the person to be addicted to sloth and gluttony, selfish in almost everything, and seldom inclined to be nice or careful in point of dress.

18. A mole on either hip shows that the person will have many children, and that such of them as survive will be healthful, lusty, and patient in all hardships.

19. A mole on the right thigh shows that the person will become rich, and also fortunate in marriage.

20. A mole on the left thigh denotes that the person suffers much by poverty and want of friends, as also by the enmity and injustice of others.

21. A mole on the right knee signifies that the person will be fortunate in the choice of a partner for life, and meet with few disappointments in the world.

22. A mole on the left knee portends that the person will be rash, inconsiderate and hasty, but modest when in cool blood, honest, and inclined to good behavior.

23. A mole on either leg shows that the person is indolent, thoughtless, and indifferent as to whatever may happen.

24. A mole on either ankle denotes a man to be inclined to effeminacy and elegancy of dress; a lady, to be courageous, active, and industrious, with some spice of the termagant.

———

Various are the opinions of authors respecting this art of divination by moles, but the above-mentioned definitions appear to me to come as near the truth as possible. However, the best way of giving judgment upon the fate of any native is first to duly examine the face of the heavens at the time of their birth; then, secondly, judge the same by their whole assemblage of features, contained in the never-failing and well-established rules of physiognomy; then, thirdly, by comparing your said judgment in all the above-mentioned sciences with this said prognostication of moles; you will then see how they agree in respect to their several accounts, which are thus to be derived from them, always remembering that the major number of testimonies and the most votes will always carry the day.

A LENT CHARM.

—

To be tried on any Friday in Lent, Good Friday excepted, when it is improper to try anything of the kind, and the mind ought to be more seriously disposed. Write twelve letters of the common alphabet on several pieces of card, also twelve figures, and the same number of blank cards; then put them in a bag and shake them well, and let each present draw one; a blank shows a single life; a figure, intrigue, or crim. con.; and a letter, a happy marriage.

CARDS.

—

How to Tell a Person's Fortune by Cards.

—

As many of those events about to happen may be easily gathered from the cards, we have here affixed the definition which each card in the pack bears separately; by combining them the reader must judge for himself, observing the following directions in laying them out: First, the person whose fortune is to be told, if a man, must choose one of the four kings to represent himself— if a woman, she must select one of the queens; the chosen card will stand for the husband or wife, mistress or lover of the party whose fortune is to be told, and the knave of the suit for the most intimate person of their family; you must then shuffle and cut the cards well, and let the person whose fortune is to be ascertained cut them three times, showing the bottom card; this must be repeated three times; then shuffle them again, let them be cut once, and display them in rows on a table, taking care always to have an odd number in each row, nine is the right number, and to place your cards exactly under each other; after this consult the situation in which the person stands by the definition we have here annexed to each card, and after having repeated it three times, form your conclusion, remember that everything is within your circle as far as you can count thirteen any way from the card that represents the person, his wife, or her husband, and their intimate friend; and also that the thirteenth card every way is of the greatest consequence, either the whole pack, or only the picked cards may be used.

Another mode with the picked cards is to shuffle and cut them, take three cards from the top—if there be two of a suit, take out the highest card; if three, take all; when you have gone through the pack, shuffle and cut the remainder, and do as before, and repeat the same a third time; then take a general view of all the cards drawn, and next couple them, a top and bottom card, then shuffle and cut them into three heaps, laying one apart in the first round to form a fourth heap; the first heap at the left hand relates to yourself entirely, the next to your family, and the third is the confirmation of the former two; you must proceed a second and third time, adding each time one to the single card, then three single cards gives the connection of the operation; observe you must add the card which represents the person whose fortune is consulted to the three, if it be not there already.

—

THE ACE OF CLUBS.—Promises great wealth, much prosperity in life, and tranquility of mind.

THE KING OF CLUBS.—Announces a man who is humane, upright, affectionate, and faithful in all his engagements; he will be very happy himself, and make every one with whom he has connection so, if he can.

THE QUEEN OF CLUBS.—Shows a tender, mild, and rather amorous disposition; one that will probably yield her maiden person to a generous lover before the matrimonial knot be tied; but that they will be happy, love each other, and be married.

THE KNAVE OF CLUBS.—Shows a generous, sincere, and zealous friend, who will exert himself warmly for your interest and welfare.

THE TEN OF CLUBS.—Denotes great riches to come speedily from an unexpected quarter; but it also threatens that you will at the same time lose some very dear friend.

THE NINE OF CLUBS.—Shows that you will displease some of your friends by too steady an adherence to your own way of thinking, nor will your success in the undertaking reconcile them to you, or procure you your own approbation.

THE EIGHT OF CLUBS.—Shows the person to be covetous, and extremely fond of money; that he will obtain it, but that it will rather prove a torment than a comfort to him, as he will not make proper use of it.

THE SEVEN OF CLUBS.—Promises the most brilliant fortune, and the most exquisite bliss that this world can afford; but beware of the opposite sex, from them alone you can experience misfortune.

THE SIX OF CLUBS.—Shows you will engage in a very lucrative partnership, and that your children will behave well.

THE FIVE OF CLUBS.—Declares that you will be shortly married to a person who will mend your circumstances.

THE FOUR OF CLUBS.—Shows incontinence for the sake of money, and frequent change of object.

THE THREE OF CLUBS.—Shows that you will be three times married, and each time to a wealthy person. This card will equally answer for a woman's being kept by three rich men according to her station.

THE DEUCE OF CLUBS.—Shows that there will be some unfortunate opposition to your favorite inclination, which will disturb you.

THE ACE OF DIAMONDS.—Shows a person who is fond of rural sports, a great builder, and a gardener; one who delights in planting and laying out groves, woods, shrubberies, and other such amusements; but that his enterprises of this nature will have success or disappointment according to the cards that are near it; it likewise signifies a letter.

THE KING OF DIAMONDS.—Shows a man of a fiery temper, preserving his anger long, seeking for opportunities of revenge, and obstinate in his resolutions.

THE QUEEN OF DIAMONDS.—Signifies that the woman will not be a steady and industrious housekeeper; that she will be fond of company, be a coquette, and not over-virtuous.

THE KNAVE OF DIAMONDS.—However nearly related, he will look more to his own interest than yours, he will be tenacious of his own opinion, and will fly off if contradicted.

THE TEN OF DIAMONDS.—Promises a country husband or a wife with great wealth and many children; the card next to it will tell the number of children; it also signifies a purse of gold.

THE NINE OF DIAMONDS.—Declares that the person will be of a roving disposition, never contented with his lot, and forever meeting with vexations and disappointments, and risks a shameful end.

THE EIGHT OF DIAMONDS.—Shows that the person, in his youth, will be an enemy to marriage, and thus run the risk of dying unmarried; but that, if he does marry, it will be late in life, and then it will be with some person whose disposition is so ill-assorted to his that it will be the cause of misfortunes.

THE SEVEN OF DIAMONDS.—Shows that you will spend your happiest days in the country, where, if you remain, your happiness will be uninterrupted; but if you come to town, you will be tormented by the infidelity of your conjugal partner, and the squandering of your substance.

THE SIX OF DIAMONDS.—Shows an early marriage and premature widowhood; but that the second marriage will probably make you worse off.

THE FIVE OF DIAMONDS.—Shows you a well-assorted marriage with a mate who will punctually perform the hymenial duties, and that you will have good children, who will keep you from grief.

THE FOUR OP DIAMONDS.—Shows the incontinence of the person you will be married to, and very great vexation to yourself, through the whole course of your life.

THE TREY OF DIAMONDS.—Shows that you will be engaged in quarrels, lawsuits, and domestic disagreements; your partner for life will be of a vixen and abusive temper, fail in the performance of the nuptial duties, and make you unhappy.

THE DEUCE OF DIAMONDS.—Shows that your heart will be engaged in love, at an early period; that your parents will not approve your choice; and that if you marry without their consent, they will hardly forgive you.

THE ACE OF HEARTS.—Signifies merrymaking, feasting, and good humor; if the ace be attended by spades, it foretells quarrelling in your cups, and ill-temper to your family while you are in a state of intoxication; if by hearts, it shows cordiality and affection between the parties; if by diamonds, your feast will be from home, perhaps in the country; if by clubs, the occasion of the meeting will be upon some bargain or agreement; if your ace of hearts is in the neighborhood of face cards of both sexes, with clubs near it, it will be about a match-making; if all the face cards are kings or knaves, or both, it will concern the buying or selling of some personal property; if all queens, it will regard conciliation between parties, and if queens and knaves, it will be about the reconciliation and reunion of a married couple.

THE KING OF HEARTS.—Shows a man of a fair complexion, of an easy and good-natured disposition, but inclined to be hasty and passionate, and rash in his undertakings.

THE QUEEN OF HEARTS.—Shows a woman of a very fair complexion, or of great beauty, her temper rather fiery, verging on the termagant, one who will not make an obedient wife, nor one who will be very happy in her own reflections.

THE KNAVE OF HEARTS.—Is a person of no particular sex, but always the dearest friend, or nearest relation of the consulting party, ever active and intruding, equally jealous of doing harm or good as the whim of the moment strikes, passionate and hard to be reconciled, but always zealous and warm in the cause of the consulting party, though probably not according to their fancy, as they will be as industrious to prevent their schemes as to forward them, if they do not accord with his own disposition. You must pay great attention to the cards that stand next to the knave, as from them alone you can judge whether the person it represents will favor your inclination or not.

THE TEN OF HEARTS.—Shows good nature and many children; it is a corrective to the bad tidings of the cards, but may stand next to it; and if its neighboring cards are of good import, it ascertains and confirms their value.

THE NINE OF HEARTS.—Promises wealth, grandeur, and high esteem; if cards that are unfavorable stand near it, you must look for disappointment and a reverse; if favorable cards follows these last at a small distance, expect to retrieve your losses, whether of peace or of goods.

THE EIGHT OF HEARTS.—Points out a strong inclination to get intoxicated; this, if accompanied with unfavorable cards, will be attended with loss of property, decay of health, and falling off of friends; if by favorable cards, it indicates reformation and recovery from the bad consequences of the former.

THE SEVEN OF HEARTS.—Shows the person to be of a fickle and unfaithful disposition, addicted to vice and incontinence, and subject to the mean art of recrimination, to excuse themselves, although without foundation.

THE SIX OF HEARTS.—Shows a generous, open, and credulous disposition, easily imposed upon, and ever the dupe of flatterers, but the good-natured friends of the distressed. If this card comes before your king or queen, you will be the dupe; if after, you will have the better.

THE FIVE OF HEARTS.—Shows a wavering unsteady disposition, never attached to one object, and free from any violent passion or attachment.

THE FOUR OF HEARTS.—Shows that the person will not be married until very late in life, and that this will probably proceed from too great a delicacy in making a choice.

THE TREY OF HEARTS.—Shows that your own imprudence will greatly contribute to your experiencing the ill-will of others.

THE DEUCE OF HEARTS.—Shows that extraordinary success and good fortune will attend the person, though, if unfavorable cards attend, this will be a long time delayed.

THE ACE OF SPADES.—Totally relates to the affairs of love, without specifying whether lawful or unlawful.

THE KING OF SPADES.—Shows a man who is ambitious, and certainly successful at court, or with some great man who will have it in his power to advance him; but let him beware of reverse.

THE QUEEN OF SPADES.—Shows a person who will be corrupted by the great of both sexes; if she is handsome, great attempts will be made on her virtue.

THE KNAVE OF SPADES.—Shows a person who, although they have your welfare at heart, will be too indolent to pursue it with zeal, unless you take frequent opportunities of rousing their attention.

THE TEN OF SPADES.—Is a card of bad import, it will, in a great measure, counteract the good effect of the other cards; but unless it be seconded by other unfortunate cards, its influence may be gotten over.

THE NINE OF SPADES.—Is the worst card in the whole pack; it portends dangerous sickness, a total loss of fortune, cruel calamity, and endless dissension in your family.

THE EIGHT OF SPADES.—Shows that you will experience strong opposition from your friends, whom you imagine to be such; if this card comes close to you, abandon your enterprise and adopt another plan.

THE SEVEN OF SPADES.—Shows the loss of a most valuable friend, whose death will plunge you into very great distress.

THE SIX OF SPADES.—Announces a mediocrity of fortune, and very great uncertainty in your undertakings.

THE FIVE OF SPADES.—Will give very little interruption to your success; it promises you good luck in the choice of a companion for life, that you will meet with one very fond of you, and immoderately attached to the joys of hymen, but shows your temper to be rather sullen.

THE FOUR OF SPADES.—Shows speedy sickness, and that your friends will injure your fortune.

THE TREY OF SPADES.—Shows that you will be unfortunate in marriage, that your partner will be incontinent, and that you will be made unhappy.

THE DEUCE OF SPADES.—Always signifies a coffin, but whom it is for must depend entirely on the other cards that are near.

Miscellaneous Games with Cards.

—

LOVER'S HEARTS.

Four persons, but not more, may play at this game; or three, by making a dumb hand, or sleeping partner, as at whist. Play this game exactly the same in every game, making the queen, whom you call Venus, above the ace, the aces in this game only standing for one. and hearts must be first led off by the person next, the dealer. He or she who gets most tricks this way (each taking up their own, and no partnership) will have most lovers, and the king and queen of hearts in one hand shows matrimony at hand. But woe to the unlucky one who gets no tricks at the deal, or does not hold a heart in their hand; they will be unfortunate in love, and long tarry before they marry.

—

CUPID AND HYMEN.

Three are enough for this game, the nines, the threes, and the aces; deal them equally; those who hold kings hold friends; queens are rivals; knaves, shame; knave alone, lover; three, surprises; ace, sorrow; two together, shows a child before marriage; if a king alone is in her hand with the aces, she stands a good chance; but if a queen is with him, she will never marry the father; the nine of hearts gives the wish that you have most at heart; the nine of diamonds, money; and the nine of clubs, a new gown or coat; but the nine of spades is sorrow. A queen and a knave in one hand bids fair for a secret intrigue.

———

HYMEN'S LOTTERY

Let each one present deposit any sum agreed on—but, of course, some trifle; put a complete pack of cards, well shuffled, in a bag or reticule. Let the party stand in a circle, and the bag being handed round, each draw three. Pairs of any kind are favorable omens of some good fortune about to occur to the party, and gets from the pool the sum back that each agreed to pay. The king of hearts is here made the god of love, and claims double, and gives a faithful swain to the fair one who has the good fortune to draw him; if Venus, the queen of hearts, is with him, it is the conquering prize, and clears the pool; fives and nines are reckoned crosses and misfortunes, and pay a forfeit of the sum agreed on to the pool, besides the usual stipend at each new game; three nines at one draw, shows the lady will be an old maid; three fives, a bad husband.

———

MATRIMONY

Let three, five, or seven young women stand in a circle and draw a card out of a box, she who gets the highest card will be married first of the company, whether she be at the present time maid, wife, or widow; and she who has the lowest, has the longest time to stay ere the sun shines on her wedding-day; she who draws the ace of spades will never bear the name of wife; and she who has the nine of hearts in this trial will have one lover too many, to her sorrow.

—

CUPID'S PASTIME

By this game you may amuse yourself and friends, and at the same time learn some curious particulars of your future fate; and though apparently a simple, yet it is a sure method, as several young persons have acknowledged to the sybil who first presented them with the rules.

Several may play at the game, it requiring no number, only leaving out nine on their board, not exposed to view; each person puts a half-penny in the pool, and the dealer double. The ace of diamonds is made principal, and takes all the other aces, etc., like Pam at Loo; twos and threes in your hand are luck; four a continuance in your present state; five, trouble; sixes, profit; sevens, plague; eights, disappointment; nines, surprises; tens, settlement; knaves, sweethearts; kings and queens, friends and acquaintances; ace of spades, death; ace of clubs, a letter; and the ace of diamonds, with ten of hearts, marriage.

The ace of diamonds being played first, or, if it be not cut, the dealer calls for the queen of hearts, which takes next; if the ace be not cut, and the queen conquers, the person who played her will marry that year without a doubt, though it may, perhaps, seem unlikely at the time; but, if she loses her queen, she must wait longer; the ace and queen being called, the rest go in rotation, as at whist, kings taking queens, queens taking knaves, and so on, and the more tricks you have, the more money you get off the board on the division after each game; those who hold the nine of spades will soon have trouble, and they are also to pay a penny to the board; but the fortunate fair one who holds the queen and knave of hearts in the same hand will soon be married, or, if she is already within the pale of matrimony, she will have a great rise in life by means of her husband; those who hold the ace of diamonds and queen of hearts clear the money off the board and end that game; it also betokens great prosperity.

Fortune-Telling by Court Cards.

—

A number of court cards is good; it tells a meeting or company—if diamonds lay next to them, it is mirth; hearts, a wedding or christening; clubs, business; and spades, a funeral. A. king and queen singly together, a courtship or wedding; a queen and knave, intrigue; and if spades are near them, the result will be disgrace, and food for scandal; the knaves together, treachery, or a suit at law; but the knave of hearts stands for Cupid, and you must find out his errand by the cards round him.

TENS.—These show changes: diamonds, unexpected luck; hearts, a removal; spades, death, or a strange bed according to the next cards; clubs, a new way of life; three or four tens, a very great surprise; two together, a visit into the country.

NINES.—The nine of spades is the worst harbinger of misfortune in the whole selected pack, it foretells a great evil; the nine of clubs is good for married women, but to single ones it tells what is usually called a love child; nine of diamonds is good for traders, and the nine of hearts for lovers and widows together; they tell changes.

SEVENS.—Ill-luck. The seven of clubs in the pack with yourself shows a drunken husband; hearts, perfidy in love or friendship; diamonds, losses; spades, scandal; three sevens together, an accident; two, imprisonment; four, danger.

THE ACES.—These vary their meaning according to their situation, turned up singly on the pack. In cutting the cards, the ace of hearts is a rich lover; in the same pack with yourself, a house, if not a ship; ace of diamonds, on the pack, a ring; with yourself, a present; in any other pack or parcel, a sum of money; club is always a busy ace, telling news, letters, or new work, let it be placed as it may. The ace of spades turned up is an unlucky prognostic; with another spade, death; with clubs, a loss in trade; with diamonds, loss of money; with hearts, unhappy marriage. The four aces together, a good settlement; three, a pleasing surprise; and two, an unpleasant one. The ace of diamonds and ten of hearts together betokens marriage, and in the pack that betokens your secret wishes; to have either of the tens or aces, or the nine of hearts, tells success, and that your desires will be speedily accomplished.

To See a Future Husband.

On midsummer eve, just after sunset, three, five, or seven young women are to go into a garden in which there is no person, and each to gather a sprig of red sage, and then, going into a room by themselves, set a stool in the middle of the room, and on it a clean basin full of rose-water, in which the sprigs of sage are to be put, and, tying a line across the room and on one side of the stool, each woman is to hang on it a clean shift turned the wrong side outward; then all are to sit down in a row, on the opposite side of the stool, as far distant as the room will admit, not speaking a single word the whole time whatever they may see, and in a few minutes after twelve each one's future husband will take her sprig out of the rosewater, and sprinkle her shift with it.

The

ORACULUM;

—or—

Napoleon Bonaparte's

BOOK OF FATE.

———

The book of which the following is a translation was obtained from Bonaparte's Cabinet of Curiosities at Leipsic during the confusion which reigned there after the defeat of the French Army. It was held by him as a sacred treasure; and it is said to have been a stimulus to most of his speculations, he being used to consult it on every occasion. The translator has several times consulted it for his own amusement; and, however, incredible it may appear, he found its answers to correspond with truth, as they afterwards came to pass. The other matters, besides obtaining a knowledge of any understanding, or an answer to a question you propose, are really curious and useful; and such, it is presumed, as are not to be found in any work in the English language. The whole forming a Cabinet of Curiosities and valuable secrets, which have been approved of by persons of respectable literary character.

———

METHOD OF WORKING THE QUESTIONS.

Make marks in the following manner, either more or less, in the four lines:

* * * * * * * * * * * *

* * * * * * * * * * * * * *

* * * * * * * * * * * * * *

* * * * * * * * * * * * * * *

This done, you will begin to reckon the number of marks in each line, from left to right; and, if the number be odd, you must mark down one dot; and if even, two dots. When the number of marks in any of the lines exceeds nine, the surplus only must be taken notice of.

The number of marks in the first line of the forgoing is odd...*
The number of marks in the second, even. ....**
The number of marks in the third, odd.........................*
The number of marks in the fourth, even...................**

———

To obtain the answer to your question you must refer to the Oraculum Table, at the top of which you will find a column of dots similar to those; you have produced. Guide your eye down the same column until you come to the letter ranging with the figure of the question you are trying; refer to the column having the same letter at the top; and, even with the dots corresponding with yours, is the answer to your question.

The following are unlucky days, on which none of the questions should be worked, or any enterprise undertaken: January 1, 2, 4; 6, 10, 20, 22; February 6, 17, 28; March 24, 26; April 10, 27, 28; May 7, 8; June 27; July 17, 21; August 20, 22; September 5, 30; October 6; November 3, 29; December 6, 10, 15.

N. B.—It is not right to try a question twice on the same day.

ORACULUM TABLE

Number	QUESTIONS.																	Number
1	Shall I obtain my wish?.......	A	B	C	D	E	F	G	H	I	K	L	M	N	O	P	Q	1
2	Success in my undertakings?..	B	C	D	E	F	G	H	I	K	L	M	N	O	P	Q	A	2
3	Shall I gain or lose my cause?.	C	D	E	F	G	H	I	K	L	M	N	O	P	Q	A	B	3
4	Shall I live in foreign parts?..	D	E	F	G	H	I	K	L	M	N	O	P	Q	A	B	C	4
5	Will the stranger return?	E	F	G	H	I	K	L	M	N	O	P	Q	A	B	C	D	5
6	Shall I recover my property?..	F	G	H	I	K	L	M	N	O	P	Q	A	B	C	D	E	6
7	Will my friend be true?.......	G	H	I	K	L	M	N	O	P	Q	A	B	C	D	E	F	7
8	Shall I have to travel?.......	H	I	K	L	M	N	O	P	Q	A	B	C	D	E	F	G	8
9	Does the person love me?.....	I	K	L	M	N	O	P	Q	A	B	C	D	E	F	G	H	9
10	Will the marriage be happy?..	K	L	M	N	O	P	Q	A	B	C	D	E	F	G	H	I	10
11	What sort of wife or husband?	L	M	N	O	P	Q	A	B	C	D	E	F	G	H	I	K	11
12	Have a son or daughter?......	M	N	O	P	Q	A	B	C	D	E	F	G	H	I	K	L	12
13	Will the patient recover?......	N	O	P	Q	A	B	C	D	E	F	G	H	I	K	L	M	13
14	Will prisoner be released?.....	O	P	Q	A	B	C	D	E	F	G	H	I	K	L	M	N	14
15	Lucky or unlucky this day?...	P	Q	A	B	C	D	E	F	G	H	I	K	L	M	N	O	15
16	What does my dream signify?	Q	A	B	C	D	E	F	G	H	I	K	L	M	N	O	P	16

	A		B
* * * *	What you wish for you will shortly obtain.	* * * *	The luck that is ordained for you will be coveted by others.
** * ** *	Signifies trouble and sorrow.	** * ** *	Whatever your desires are, for the present decline them.

* ** * *	Be very cautious what you do this day, lest trouble befall you.	* ** * *	Signifies a favor or kindness from some person.
** * * **	The prisoner dies, and is regretted by his friends.	** * * **	There are enemies, who would defraud and render you unhappy.
** ** ** *	Life will be spared this time, to prepare for death.	** ** ** *	With great difficulty he will obtain pardon or release again.
** ** * **	A very handsome daughter, but a painful one.	** ** * **	The patient should be prepared to leave this world.
** * * *	You will have a virtuous and religious woman or man for your wife or husband.	** * * *	She will have a son, who will be learned and wise.
** ** * *	If you marry this person, you will have enemies where you little expect.	** ** * *	A rich partner is ordained for you.
* * ** **	You had better decline this love, for it is neither constant nor true.	* * ** **	By this marriage you will have great luck and prosperity.
* * *	Decline your travels, for they will not be to your advantage.	* * *	This love comes from an upright and sincere heart.

**		**	
** * ** **	There is a true and sincere friendship between you both.	** * ** **	God will surely travel with you and bless you.
* ** ** **	You will not recover the stolen property.	* ** ** **	Beware of friends who are false and deceitful.
* ** ** *	The stranger will, with joy, soon return.	* ** ** *	You will recover your property unexpectedly.
* * ** *	You will not recover the stolen property.	* * ** *	Love prevents his return home at present.
* ** * **	The Lord will support you in a good cause.	* ** * **	Your stay is not here; be, therefore, prepared for a change.
** ** ** **	You are not lucky—pray to God that he may help you.	** ** ** **	You will have no gain; therefore be wise and careful.
C		**D**	
* * * *	With the blessing of God, you will have great gain.	* * * *	You will obtain a great fortune in another country.

** * ** *	Very unlucky indeed; pray to God for his assistance.	** * ** *	By venturing freely, you will certainly gain doubly.
* ** * *	If your desires are not extravagant, they will be granted.	* ** * *	God will change your misfortune into success and happiness.
** * * **	Signifies peace and plenty between friends.	** * * **	Alter your intentions, or else you may meet poverty and distress.
** ** ** *	Be well prepared this day, or you may meet with trouble.	** ** ** *	Signifies that you have many impediments in the accomplishment of your pursuits.
** ** * **	The prisoner will find it difficult to obtain his pardon or release.	** ** * **	Whatever may possess your inclinations this day, abandon them.
** * * *	The patient will yet enjoy health and prosperity.	** * * *	The prisoner will get free again this time.
** ** * *	She will have a daughter, and will require attention.	** ** * *	The patient's illness will be lingering and doubtful.
* * **	The person has not a great fortune, but is in middling circumstances.	* * **	She will have a dutiful and handsome son.

**		**	
* * * **	Decline this marriage, or else you may be sorry.	* * * **	The person will be low in circumstances, but honest-hearted.
** * ** **	Decline a courtship which may be your destruction.	** * ** **	A marriage which will add to your welfare and prosperity.
* ** ** **	Your travels are in vain; you had better stay at home.	* ** ** **	You love a person who does not speak well of you.
* ** ** *	You may depend on a true and sincere friendship.	* ** ** *	Your travels will be prosperous, if guided by prudence.
* * ** *	You must not expect to regain that which you have lost.	* * ** *	He means not what he says, for his heart is false.
* ** * **	Sickness prevents the traveller from seeing you.	* ** * **	With some trouble and expense, you may gain your properly.
** ** ** **	It will be your fate to stay where you now are.	** ** ** **	You must not expect to see the Stranger again.

E		F	
* * * *	The stranger will not return so soon as you expect.	* * * *	By persevering, you will recover your property.
** * ** *	You have no luck; pray to God, and strive honestly.	** * ** *	It is out of the stranger's power to return.
* ** * *	You will hereafter gain what you seek.	* ** * *	You will gain, and be successful in foreign parts.
** * * **	Remain among your friends, and you will do well.	** * * **	A great fortune is ordained for you, wait patiently.
** ** ** *	You will obtain your wishes by means of a friend.	** ** ** *	There is great hindrance to your success at present.
** ** * **	Signifies that you have enemies, who will endeavor to ruin, and make you unhappy.	** ** * **	Your wishes are in vain at present.
** * * *	Beware: an enemy is endeavoring to bring you to strife and misfortune.	** * * *	Signifies there is danger and sorrow before you.
**	The prisoner's sorrow and	**	This day is unlucky;

** * *	anxiety are great, and his release uncertain.	** * *	therefore, alter your intention.
* * ** **	The patient will soon recover; there is no danger.	* * ** **	The prisoner will be restored to liberty and freedom.
* * * **	She will have a daughter, who will be honored and respected.	* * * **	The patient's recovery is doubtful.
** * ** **	Your partner will be fond of liquor, and will debase himself or herself thereby.	** * ** **	She will have a very fine boy.
* ** ** **	This marriage will bring you to poverty; be, therefore, discreet.	* ** ** **	A worthy person, and a fine fortune.
* ** ** *	Their love is false to you and true to others.	* ** ** *	Your intentions would destroy your rest and peace.
* * ** *	Decline your travels for the present, for they will be dangerous.	* * ** *	This love is true and constant; forsake it not.
* ** * **	This person is serious and true, and deserves to be respected.	* ** * **	Proceed on your travels or journey, and you will not have cause to repent it.

** ** ** **	You will not recover the property you have lost.	** ** ** **	If you trust this friend, you may have cause for sorrow.
	G		**H**
* * * *	This friend exceeds all others in every respect.	* * * *	Commence your travels, and they will go on as you could wish.
** * ** *	You must bear your loss with fortitude.	** * ** *	Your pretended friend hates you secretly.
* ** * *	The stranger will return unexpectedly.	* ** * *	Your hopes to recover your property are vain.
** * * **	Remain at home among your friends and you will escape misfortunes.	** * * **	A certain affair prevents the stranger's return immediately.
** ** ** *	You will meet no gain in your pursuits.	** ** ** *	Your fortune you will find in abundance abroad.
** ** * **	Heaven will bestow its blessings on you.	** ** * **	Decline the pursuit and you will do well.
**	No.	**	Your expectations are vain;

* * *		* * *	you will not succeed.
** ** * *	Signifies that you will shortly be out of the power of your enemies.	** ** * *	You will obtain what you wish for.
* * ** **	Ill-luck awaits you; it will be difficult for you to escape it.	* * ** **	Signifies that this day your fortune will change for the better.
* * * **	The prisoner will be released by death only.	* * * **	Cheer up your spirits, your luck is at hand.
** * ** **	By the blessing of God, the patient will recover.	** * ** **	After long imprisonment he will be released.
* ** ** **	A daughter, but of a very weakly constitution.	* ** ** **	The patient will be relieved from sickness.
* ** ** *	You will get an honest, young and handsome partner.	* ** ** *	She will have a healthy son.
* * ** *	Decline this marriage, else it may be to your sorrow.	* * ** *	You will be married to your equal in a short time.

* ** * **	Avoid this love.	* ** * **	If you wish to be happy, do not marry this person.
** ** ** **	Prepare for a short journey; you will be recalled by an unexpected event.	** ** ** **	This love is from the heart, and will continue until death.
I		**K**	
* * * *	The love is great, but will cause great jealousy.	* * * *	After much misfortune you will be comfortable and happy.
** * ** *	It will be in vain for you to travel.	** * ** *	A sincere love from an upright heart.
* ** * *	Your friend will be as sincere as you could wish him to be.	* ** * *	You will be prosperous in your journey.
** * * **	You will recover the stolen property through a cunning person.	** * * **	Do not rely on the friendship of this person.
** ** ** *	The traveller will soon return with joy.	** ** ** *	The property is lost forever, but the thief will be punished.
**	You will not be prosperous	**	The traveller will be absent

** * **	or fortunate in foreign parts.	** * **	some considerable time.
** * * *	Place your trust in God, who is the disposer of happiness.	** * * *	You will meet luck and happiness in a for-_ eign country.
** ** * *	Your fortune will shortly be changed into misfortune.	** ** * *	You will not have any success for the present.
* * ** **	You will succeed as you desire.	* * ** **	You will succeed in your undertaking.
* * * **	Signifies the misfortune which threatens will be prevented.	* * * **	Change your intentions and you will do well.
** * ** **	Beware of your enemies, who seek to do you harm.	** * ** **	Signifies that there are rogues at hand.
* ** ** **	After a short time your anxiety for the prisoner will cease.	* ** ** **	Be reconciled; your circumstances will shortly mend.
* ** ** *	God will give the patient health and strength again.	* ** ** *	The prisoner will be released.

* * ** *	She will have a very fine daughter.	* * ** *	The patient will depart this life.
* ** * **	You will marry a person with whom you will have little comfort.	* ** * **	She will have a son.
** ** ** **	The marriage will not answer your expectations.	** ** ** **	It will be difficult for you to get a partner.
L		**M**	
* * * *	You will get a very handsome person for your partner.	* * * *	She will have a son, who will gain wealth and honor.
** * ** *	Various misfortunes will attend this marriage.	** * ** *	She will get a partner with great undertakings and much money.
* ** * *	This love is whimsical and changeable.	* ** * *	The marriage will be prosperous.
** * * **	You will he unlucky in your travels.	** * * **	She, or he, wishes to he yours this moment.
**	This person's love is just	**	Your journey Will prove to

** ** *	and true. You may rely on it.	** ** *	your advantage.
** ** * **	You will lose, hut the thief will suffer most.	** ** * **	Place no great trust in that person.
** * * *	The stranger will soon return with plenty.	** * * *	You will find your property at a certain time.
** ** * *	If you remain at home, you will have success.	** ** * *	The traveller's return is rendered doubtful by his conduct.
* * ** **	Your gain will he trivial.	* * ** **	You will succeed as you desire in foreign parts.
* * * **	You will meet with sorrow and trouble.	* * * **	Expect no gain; it will be in vain.
** * ** **	You will succeed according to your wishes.	** * ** **	You will have more luck than you expect.
* ** ** **	Signifies that you will get money.	* ** ** **	Whatever your desires are, you will speedily obtain them.

* ** ** *	In spite of enemies, you will do well.	* ** ** *	Signifies you will be asked to a wedding.
* * ** *	The prisoner will pass many days in confinement.	* * ** *	You will have no occasion to complain of ill-luck.
* ** * **	The patient will recover.	* ** * **	Some one will pity and release the prisoner.
** ** ** **	She will have a daughter.	** ** ** **	The patient's recovery is unlikely.
N		**O**	
* * * *	The patient will recover, but his days are short.	* * * *	The prisoner will be released with joy.
** * ** *	She will have a daughter.	** * ** *	The patient's recovery is doubtful.
* ** * *	You will marry into a very respectable family.	* ** * *	She will have a son, who will live to a great age.
**	By this marriage you will	**	You will get a virtuous

* * **	gain nothing.	* * **	partner.
** ** ** *	Await the time and you will find the love great.	** ** ** *	Delay not this marriage; you will meet much happiness.
** ** * **	Venture not from home.	** ** * **	None loves you better in this world.
** * * *	This person is a sincere friend.	** * * *	You may proceed with confidence.
** ** * *	You will never recover the theft.	** ** * *	Not a friend, but a secret enemy.
* * ** **	The stranger will return, but not quickly.	* * ** **	You will soon recover what is stolen.
* * * **	When abroad, keep from evil women, or they will do you harm.	* * * **	The stranger will not return.
** * ** **	You will soon gain what you little expect.	** * ** **	A foreign woman will greatly enhance your fortune.

* ** ** **	You will have great success.	* ** ** **	You will be cheated out of your gain.
* ** ** *	Rejoice ever at that which is ordained for you.	* ** ** *	Your misfortunes will vanish and you will be happy.
* * ** *	Signifies that sorrow will depart and joy will return.	* * ** *	Your hope is in vain; fortune shuns you at present.
* ** * **	Your luck is in blossom; it will soon be at hand.	* ** * **	That you will soon hear agreeable news.
** ** ** **	Death may end the imprisonment.	** ** ** **	There are misfortunes lurking about you.
P		**Q**	
* * * *	This day brings you an increase of happiness.	* * * *	Signifies much joy and happiness between friends.
** * ** *	The prisoner will escape from his enemies.	** * ** *	This day is not very lucky, but rather the reverse.
*	The patient will recover	*	He will yet come to honor,

** * *	and live long.	** * *	although he now suffers.
** * * **	She will have two daughters.	** * * **	Recovery is doubtful, therefore be prepared for the worst.
** ** ** *	A rich, young person will be your partner.	** ** ** *	She will have a son, who will prove froward.
** ** * **	Hasten your marriage; it will bring you much happiness.	** ** * **	A rich partner, but a bad temper.
** * * *	The person loves you sincerely.	** * * *	By wedding this person you ensure your happiness.
** ** * *	You will not prosper from home.	** ** * *	The person has great love for you, but wishes to conceal it.
* * ** **	This friend is more valuable than gold.	* * ** **	You may proceed on your journey without fear.
* * * **	You will never receive your goods.	* * * **	Trust him not; he is inconstant and deceitful.

** * ** **	He is dangerously ill, and cannot yet return.	** * ** **	In a very singular manner yon will recover your property.
* ** ** **	Depend upon your own industry, and remain at home.	* ** ** **	The stranger will return very soon.
* ** ** *	Be joyful, for future prosperity is ordained for you.	* ** ** *	You will dwell abroad in comfort and happiness.
* * ** *	Depend not too much on your good luck.	* * ** *	If you deal fairly, you will surely prosper.
* ** * **	What you wish will be granted to you.	* ** * **	You will yet live in splendor and plenty.
** ** ** **	That you should be very careful this day, lest any accident befall you.	** ** ** **	Make yourself contented with your present fortune.

Fortune-Telling
—by the—
Grounds of a Coffee or Tea Cup.

—

Pour the grounds of coffee or tea into a white cup; shake them well about in it, so that their particles may cover the surface of the whole cup; then reverse it into the saucer, that all the superfluous parts may be drained off, and the figures required for fortune-telling be formed.

It is not to be expected upon taking up the cup that the figures will be accurately represented as they are in the cards, but it is quite sufficient if they bear some resemblance to any of the thirty-two emblems; and the more fertile the fancy shall be of the person who inspects the cup, the more he will discover in it.

THE ROADS, or serpentine lines, indicate ways; if they are covered with clouds, and consequently in the thick, they are said to be infallible marks of many past or future reverses. But if they appear in the clear and serene, are the surest tokens of some fortunate change near at hand; encompassed with many points or dots, they signify an accidental gain of money; likewise long life.

THE RING signifies marriage; if a letter is near it, it denotes to the person that has his fortune told the initial of the name of the party to be married. If the ring is in the clear, it portends happy and lucrative friendship. Surrounded with clouds, denotes that the party is to use precaution in the friendship he is about to contract, lest he should be insidiously deceived; but it is most inauspicious if the ring appears at the bottom of the cup, as it forebodes an entire separation from the beloved object.

THE LEAF OF CLOVER may be generally considered a lucky sign. Its different disposition in the cup alone makes the difference. When it is on the top it shows that the good fortune is not far distant, but it is subject to delay, if it is in the middle or at the bottom. Should clouds surround it, it shows that many disagreeable circumstances attend the good fortune; in the clear, it prognosticates serene and undisturbed happiness as the party wishes.

THE ANCHOR, the emblem of hope and commerce, implies successful business carried on by water and by land, if on the bottom of the cup; at the top, and in the clear part, it shows constant love and unshaken fidelity. In thick and cloudy parts it also denotes love, but tinctured with the inconstancy of the butterfly.

THE SERPENT—Always the emblem of falsehood and enmity—is likewise the general sign of an enemy. On the top or in the middle of the cup, it promises to the consulting party the triumph which he desires over his enemy; but he will not obtain it so easily if the serpent be in the thick and cloudy part. By the letter which appears near the emblem the enemy may easily be guessed, as it makes the initial of his name.

THE LETTER.—By letters we communicate to our friends either pleasant or unpleasant news, and such is the case here; if this emblem is in the clear part, it denotes the speedy arrival of welcome news; surrounded with, dots, it announces the arrival of a considerable remittance of money; but hemmed in by clouds, it is quite the contrary, and forebodes some melancholy or bad tidings, a loss, or some other sinister accident. If it be in the clear, and accompanied with a heart, lovers may expect a letter which secures to the party the possession of the beloved object; but in the thick, it denotes a refusal.

THE COFFIN, the emblem of death, prognosticates the same thing here, or at least a long and tedious illness; if it be in the thick at the top of the cup, it signifies a considerable estate left by some rich relation; in the same manner at the bottom, shows that the deceased is not so nearly related to the consulting party.

THE STAR denotes happiness, if in the clear and at the top of the cup; clouded, or in the thick, it signifies long life, though exposed to various troubles. If dots are about it, it foretells great fortune, wealth, high respectability, honors, etc. Several stars denote some good and happy children, but, surrounded with dashes, shows that the person's children will cause him or her grief and vexation in old age, and that you ought to prevent it by giving them a good education in time.

THE DOG, being at all times the emblem of faithfulness or envy, has a two-fold meaning here. At the top, in the clear, it signifies true and faithful friends; but if his image be surrounded with clouds and dashes, it shows that those whom you take for your friends are not to be depended on; but if the dog be at the bottom of the cup, you have to dread the effects of extreme envy or jealousy.

THE LILY.—If this emblem be at the top, or in the middle of the cup, it signifies that the consulting party either has, or will have, a virtuous spouse; if it be at the bottom, it denotes quite the reverse. In the clear, the lily further betokens long and happy life; if clouded, or in the thick, it portends trouble and vexation, especially on the part of one's relations.

THE CROSS, be it one or more, generally predicts adversities; its position varies, and so do the circumstances. If it be at the top, and in the clear, it shows that the misfortunes of the party will soon be at an end, or that he will easily get over them; but if it appears in the middle or at the bottom of the thick, the party must expect some severe trials. If it appears with dots, either in the clear or the thick, it promises a speedy change in one's sorrow.

THE CLOUDS.—If they be more light than dark, the person will have a good result from wishing, but, if black, it must be given up. Surrounded with dots, they bring success in trade, and in all undertakings; but the brighter they are the greater will be the happiness.

THE SUN, an emblem of the greatest luck and happiness, if in the clear; but in the thick it denotes a great deal of sadness; surrounded by dots and dashes, denotes an alteration will speedily take place.

THE MOON, if it appears in the clear, denotes high honors; in the dark or thick part it implies sadness, which will, however, pass without great prejudice; but if it be at the bottom of the cup, the consulting person will be fortunate on water and land.

MOUNTAIN.—If it represent only one mountain, it indicates the favor of people of high rank, but several of them, especially in the thick, are signs of powerful enemies; if in the clear, denotes the contrary, or friends in high life, who are endeavoring to promote the consulting party.

TREE.—One tree only, if it be in the clear or thick part, points out lasting good health; several trees denote that your wish will be accomplished. If they are encompassed with dashes, it is a token that your fortune is in its blossom, and will require some time to bring it to maturity. If it is accompanied with dots, it is a sign that you will make a fortune at a distance off, where you will reside.

CHILD.—In the clear part it bespeaks innocent intercourse between the consulter and another person; in the thick part, excess in love affairs, attended with great expenses; at the bottom of the cup it denotes the consequences of libidinous amours.

WOMAN.—Signifies much joy in general. If in the clear, this emblem has a more favorable signification than in the thick; there it shows very great happiness, here a great deal of jealousy. If dots surround the image, it explains the lady's fertility or her wealth. The different positions in the cup shows, at the top, and in the middle, that you will be in love with a virgin, but at the bottom it marks that she is a widow.

THE PEDESTRIAN denotes, in general, a merchant, good business, pleasant news, and recovery of lost things. It also signifies that the consulting party will soon enlist, or get some engagement.

THE RIDER denotes good news from abroad in money matters, a good situation in a foreign country, or good prospects. He that doubts his fortune is promised a lasting one by this emblem.

THE MOUSE.—As this animal lives by stealth, it is also an emblem here of theft or robbery; if it is in the clear, it shows you will get again what you lost in a wonderful manner; but if it appears in the thick, you must renounce this hope.

THE ROSE, or any other flower, the greatest success in the arts and sciences; if the consulting party be married, he will have good children, and all the fruits to be expected from their good education in his old age.

THE HEART, if it be in the clear, signifies future pleasure. It promises joy at receiving some money if surrounded with dots. If a ring or two hearts be together, it signifies that the party is about to be married or betrothed; if a letter be perceptible near it, it shows the initial of a person's name; if a letter be in the clear, the party is a virgin; if in the thick, a widow.

GARDEN OR WOOD signifies a concourse of people; in the clear it indicates good friends, of which it will consist; in the thick, or encompassed with streaks, it warns the consulting person to be cautious, and not to take for his friends those who profess themselves as such.

BIRDS IN GENERAL.—In the clear, it signifies that the disagreeables and troubles with which the person shall have to combat will soon be over; in the thick, it is a sign of good living and of a successful journey or voyage, which, if there are dashes, will be directed to a great distance.

FISH IN GENERAL denotes successful events by water, if in the clear, which will either happen to the consulter, or improve the state of his affairs beyond the water. If they are in the thick, the consulter will fish in troubled water, and place his confidence upon that which others have lost before him. Surrounded with dots, denotes that his fate calls him to some distant place.

LION, OR ANY OTHER FEROCIOUS BEAST.—At the top, in the clear, it signifies all kinds of good luck with people of high rank; at the bottom, it warns the consulter to shun all such intercourse, as he will, at all events, find persons who will be envious of his fortune, and not see it with indifference.

GREEN BUSH shows the benevolence and favors of all the consumer's patrons; it gives some hopes of attaining the honor the consulter wishes for; without foliage, it is a token of the caprice of fortune; in the clear, it announces an unexpected remittance of money.

WORMS.—At the top, or in the middle of the top, it denotes good luck at gambling and in marriage; below, it warns the consulter against rivals in courtship and against enviers in trade.

HOUSE indicates, at the top of the cup, blessings and success in the consulter's enterprise; if the present situation be not the most favorable, trust that it will soon change for the better. In the middle or below, it cautions the consulter to be vigilant over servants, as vigilance alone will prevent injury.

SCYTHE, if combined with an hour-glass, denotes imminent dangers of all kinds; below, it signifies a long and prosperous life.

DREAMS, TOKENS, AND INSIGHTS

INTO FUTURITY.

—

THE RING AND OLIVE BRANCH.

Buy a ring; it matters not it being gold, so as it has the semblance of a wedding ring; and it is best to try this charm on your own birthday. Pay for your ring with some small bill, for whatever change you receive you must give it to the first beggar you meet in the street; and, if no one asks alms of you, give it to some poor person—for you need not, alas! go far before you find one to whom your charity will be acceptable; carefully note what they say in return, such as "God bless you," or wishing you luck and prosperity, as is usual. When you get home, write it down on a sheet of paper, at each of four corners, and, in the middle, put the two first letters of your name, your age, and the letters of the planets then reigning as morning and evening stars; get a branch of olive and fasten the ring on the stalk with a string of thread which has been steeped all day in a mixture of honey and vinegar, or any composition of opposite qualities, very sweet and very sour; cover your ring and stalk with the written paper, carefully wrapped round and round; wear it in your bosom till the ninth hour of the night; then repair to the next church-yard and bury the charm in the grave of a young man who died unmarried; and, while you are so doing, repeat the letters of your own Christian name three times backwards; return home, and keep as silent as possible till you go to bed, which must be before eleven; put a light in your chimney, or some safe place, and, before midnight, or just about that time, your husband that is to be will present himself at the foot of the bed, but will presently disappear. If you are not to marry, none will come; and, in that case, if you dream before morning of children, it shows that you will have them unmarried; and if you dream of crowds of men, beware of prostitution.

—

THE WITCHES' CHAIN.

Let three young women join together in making a long chain—about a yard will do—of Christmas, juniper, and mistletoe berries, and, at the end of every link, put an oak acorn. Exactly before midnight let them assemble in a room by themselves, where no one can disturb them; leave a window open, and take the key out of the keyhole and hang it over the chimney-piece; have a good fire, and place in the midst of it a long, thinnish log of wood, well sprinkled with oil, salt, and fresh mould; then wrap the chain round it, each maiden having an equal share in the business; then sit down, and on your left knee let each fair one have a prayer-book opened at the matrimonial service. Just as the last acorn is burned, the future husband will cross the room; each one will see her own proper spouse, but he will be invisible to the rest of the wakeful virgins. Those that are not to be wed will see a coffin, or some mis-shapen form cross the room; go to bed instantly, and you will all have remarkable dreams. This must be done either on a Wednesday or Friday night, but no other.

—

LOVE'S CORDIAL.

(To be tried the third night of a new moon.)

Take brandy, rum, gin, wine, and the oil of amber, of each a teaspoonful; a tablespoonful of cream, and three of spring water; drink it as you get into bed; repeat:

This mixture of love I take for my potion,
That I of my destiny may have a notion;
Cupid befriend me, new moon be kind,
And show unto me that fate that's designed.

You will dream of drink, and, according to the quality or manner of it being presented, you may tell the condition to which you will rise or fall by marriage. Water is poverty; and if you dream of a drunken man, it is ominous that you will have a drunken mate. If you dream of drinking too much, you will fall, at a future period, into that sad error yourself, without great care; and what is a worse sight than an inebriated female? She cannot guard her own honor, ruins her own and family's substance, and often clothes herself with rags. Trouble is often used as an excuse for this vicious habit; but it gives more trouble than it takes away.

—

LOVE LETTERS.

On receiving a love-letter that has any particular declaration in it, lay it wide open; then fold it in nine folds, pin it next your heart, and thus wear it till bedtime; then place it in your left-hand glove, and lay it under your head. If you dream of gold, diamonds, or any costly gems, your lover is true, and means what he says; if of white linen, you will lose him by death; and if of flowers, he will prove false. If you dream of his saluting you, he is, at present, false, and means not what he professes, but only to draw you into a snare.

—

MAGIC ROSE.

Gather your rose on the 27th of June; let it be full blown, and as bright a red as you can get; pluck it between the hours of three and four in the morning, taking care to have no witness of the transaction; convey it to your chamber, and hold it over a chaffing-dish or any convenient utensil for the purpose, in which there is charcoal and sulphur of brimstone; hold your rose over the smoke about five minutes, and you will see it have a wonderful effect on the flower. Before the rose gets the least cool, clap it in a sheet of writing-paper, on which is written your own name and that of the young man you love best; also the date of the year and the name of the morning star that has the ascendency at that time; fold it up and seal it neatly with three separate seals, then run and bury the parcel at the foot of the tree from which you gathered the flower; here let it remain untouched till the 6th of July; take it up at midnight, go to bed and place it under your pillow, and you will have a singular and most eventful dream before morning, or, at least, before your usual time of rising. You may keep the rose under your head three nights without spoiling the charm;

when you are done with the rose and paper be sure to burn them.

Good Sympathetic Ink.

—

How any Person can Write Secretly.

—

It is made by taking an ounce of common aquafortis, which you are to mix with three ounces of common water; you may use this to write on paper that is very strong and stiff; this writing becomes totally invisible in drying. In order to make it reappear, you need only wet the paper, and when it dries the writing disappears again. The effect may be repented two or three times. With this ink lovers can communicate with each other without any fear of intrusion.

Observations Concerning
BIRDS AND BEASTS.

—

It hath been duly observed by the learned in all ages of the world that our all-wise and beneficent Creator originally implanted in the frame of nature a means whereby mankind may attain to the knowledge such future contingencies as concern their welfare and happiness; and more especially since we observe, even in the brute creation, that even the most inconsiderable creatures upon the earth are more or less endowed with a gift of foreknowledge. Thus the industrious bee and the laborious ant lay in their summer store, in order to supply the necessary wants of an inclement winter, which they foreknow is yet to come; yea, even of all the whole race of reptiles, the ant, the spider, and the bee, appear to be endowed with the greatest share of sagacity.

The wisdom of the ant is conspicuous in forming themselves into a kind of republic, and therein observing, as it were, their own peculiar laws and policies; but the cunning of the spider seems to exceed that of most other insects; its various artifices to ensnare its prey are no less remarkable than its contrivance of a cell or retreat behind its web, where it feasts upon its game in safety, and conceals the fragments of those carcasses it has devoured, without exposing to public view the least remains of its barbarity which might tend to distinguish its place of abode, or create the least jealousy in any sect, that their enemy was near. Into what history can we look to find people who are governed by laws equal to what we observe in the republic of bees? What experience can we desire beyond that we observe in the cunning spider, to teach us to guard against the artifices of those who lay snares to catch the thoughtless and unwary? or what can exceed the indefatigable ant, in teaching us lessons of frugality and industry?

The badger, the hedge-hog, and the mole also provide themselves a magazine of plants and herbs, which they foreknow will enable them to lie concealed in their holes during the hard frosts of winter, contented with their prison, which affords them safety. Their holes are also constructed with amazing art, and have generally two apertures, that, in case one should be beset by an enemy, they may escape by the other.

The doublings of the hare, and the tricks of the fox, to escape the hounds, are also astonishing indications of foresight and sagacity. The feathered race are likewise endowed with a similar faculty, and often foretell an approaching storm a considerable time before it appears by retiring in flocks to their holes and hiding-places for shelter and protection. The birds of passage seem to inherit this gift in a most remarkable degree, for they assemble together in prodigious flocks at an appointed hour, and take their leave before the approach of winter, which they foresee will destroy the flies and insects, as they feed on nothing else. And it is no less extraordinary than true that these birds return as early as the sun brings forth this class of insects into new life; and they have also the sagacity to find out and possess their old nests and habitations.

This wise provident forecast for self-preservation and safety is even extended to the innumerable inhabitants of the immense ocean, where we see the fishes, pressed by unceasing hunger, indiscriminately prey upon one another—the large upon the small, even of its own species; whence the smaller fish, in regular gradations, when in danger of being devoured, fly for an asylum to the shallow waters, where they know their enemy either cannot or dare not come to pursue them. And this pursuit of one species of fish after another is by no means confined to a single region; for we find shoals of them pursuing one another, from the vicinity of the pole even down to the equator; and thus the cod from the banks of Newfoundland pursues the whiting, which, flies before it even to the southern shores of Spain. It is astonishing, also, that herrings, which appear to generate towards the north of Scotland, regularly make their way once a year to the British Channel. Their voyage is conducted with the utmost regularity, and the time of their departure is fixed from the months of June to August. They always assemble together before they set out, and no stragglers are ever found from the general body. It is impossible to assign any cause for this emigration; but it, doubtless, proceeds from the same instinctive impulse with which all orders of animated nature are more or less endued.

Now observe that when you go out of your house to do or transact any kind of business, and in the way you do see a man or a bird going or flying, so that either of them do set themselves before you on your right hand, that is a good signification in reference to your business; but when you shall go out of your house on any business whatsoever, and shall see a bird or a man before you on the left side of you, it is an ill-sign in reference to your said business.

When either a man or a bird shall thus pass before you, coming from the right side of you and bending towards the left, goeth out of your sight, that is a good sign concerning your business. When you do first find a man going, or a bird flying, and then he rests himself before you on your right side, and you seeing it, this is also a good sign of success in your business. But when you see a man or a bird bending from your right side to the left, it is an ill sign concerning your business; when a man or a bird comes behind you, and goes faster than you, but before he cometh at you he rests, or the same before you came to him, he rests, and you seeing him on your right side, it is to you a good sign. But when this-happens on the left side, it is an evil sign. When a man or a bird coming from your left side and passing to the right, goeth out of your sight without resting, it is a good sign. If a man or a bird coming from your right hand, passing behind your back to the left, and you see him resting anywhere, this is an evil sign.

All the auspicia which first happeneth in the beginning of any business ought to be taken notice of, as if in the beginning of any work you do find that rats have been gnawing your clothes, then desist from your undertakings. If at going out of your house you happen to-stumble on the threshold, or if in the way you happen to dash your foot against anything, then forbear your journey; if any ill omen ever happens at the beginning of your business, then put it off for a while, lest you be completely disappointed therein.

If a crow, raven, or a jack-daw do croak over any person, it doth show much evil of a serious nature. The magpie informs you that you will soon hear news, and come into company; but whether such news be good or bad, observe whether it comes from the right hand: or left. The screech owl is always unfortunate, for, about the 17th of October, 1807, Grantham Church was a repository for a number of owls every evening for about one month, when it followed that, before that time the next year, that same church was actually robbed of all its plate and money, to a large amount, by a gang of villains, in the dead of the night, to the great loss and detriment of the whole parish. If you meet sparrows, it is unfortunate, except for love.

Flies indicate importunity and impudent affronts; cocks meeting you, or crowing against your house, inform you of visitors coming, and success in your journeys and business. If you meet a hare, a mule, or a hog, it is an ill omen. To meet horses in a carriage is good, but if you meet an ass, expect trouble; while to meet sheep and goats is very good, and indicates prosperity in your affairs. If you either meet a dog or oxen, you may expect the same success, for it is good. Mice indicate that you will soon meet with danger; locusts making a stand in any place, hindereth a person from their wishes, and is an ill omen; on the contrary, grasshoppers promote a journey, and foretell a good event of things.

The spider weaving a line downwards signifies hope of money to come; as also the ants having a nest near your door is good, because they know how to provide for themselves, and portends security and riches. If you meet with a snake, take care of an ill-tongued enemy. A viper signifies lewd women and wicked children; an eel shows a man that is displeased with everybody.

But, of all the various auspicias and omens, there is none more effectual or potent than man, none that doth signify the truth more clearly. You must, therefore, dilligently note, and duly observe, the condition of that man you meet, or that meeteth you; his age, profession, station, gesture, motion, exercise, complexion, habit, name, words, speech, etc., for, seeing there are in all other animals so many discoveries of presages, yet those are all more efficacious and clear which are infused into the soul of man. We must also consider what animals are Saturnine, those under Jupiter, Mars, etc., and thus, according to their properties, draw forth their presages.

Fortunate Days, Weeks, Months and Years.

—

The day of the week in which you were born is the best for any person; it is lucky to receive a letter on the third, fifth, or ninth of the month, or on any Tuesday or Saturday. The first week in May is very fortunate for any undertaking to men; the second, to women. June is a good month in which to make any contract, or receive a promise of marriage, as it generally turns out sincere and prosperous.

It has often been recorded, and though a singular observation, experience has shown it to be true, that some event of importance is sure to happen to a woman in her thirty-first year, whether single or married; it may prove for her good, or it, may be some great evil or temptation; therefore, let her be cautious and circumspect in all her actions. If she is a maiden or a widow, it is probable that she marries this year.

The same is applicable to men in their forty-second year, of which many instances have been proved that do not admit of a doubt; observe, always, to grant or take a base for an odd number of years; even years are not prosperous. The three first days of the moon are the best for signing papers, and the first five days, as well as the twenty-fourth, for any fresh undertaking.

But it must be allowed that much depends on people's own industry and perseverance; that often overcomes a bad planet, or a day marked unlucky in the book of fate.

Mondays, Wednesdays and Fridays are the best for men; Tuesdays, Thursdays and Saturdays for women. To travel by land, choose the increase of the moon, the decrease for a voyage, and about the full to write letters in which you ask a favor; to beg wafers is not lucky on this occasion. It is not good to marry on your own birthday, for a woman, but is fortunate for a man; and it is good to christen a child on the day of the week in which it was born. It is also reckoned fortunate to be born on Sunday, for either sex.

DREAMS.
How to Receive Oracles by Dreams.

He who would receive true dreams, should keep a pure, undisturbed, and imaginative spirit, and so compose it that it may be made worthy of knowledge and government by the mind; for such a spirit is most fit for prophesying, and is a most clear glass of all images which flow everywhere from all things. When, therefore, we are sound in body, not disturbed in mind, our intellect not made dull by heavy meats and strong drink, not sad through poverty, not provoked through lust, not incited by any vice, nor stirred up by wrath or anger, not being irreligiously and profanely inclined, not given to levity nor lost in drunkenness, but, chastely going to bed, fall asleep, then our pure and divine soul being free from all the evils above recited, and separated from all hurtful thoughts—and now freed, by dreaming—is endowed with this divine spirit as an instrument, and doth receive those beams and representations which are darted down, as it were, and shine forth from the divine Mind into itself, in a deifying glass.

There are four kinds of true dreams, viz., the first, matutine, *i.e.,* between sleeping and waking; the second, that which one sees concerning another; the third, that whose interpretation is shown to the same dreamer in the nocturnal vision; and, lastly, that which is related to the same dreamer in the nocturnal vision. But natural things and their own co-mixtures do likewise belong unto wise men, and we often use such to receive oracles from a spirit by a dream, which are either by perfumes, unctions, meats, drinks, rings, seals, etc.

Now those who are desirous to receive oracles through a dream, let them make themselves a ring of the Sun or Saturn for this purpose. There are likewise images of dreams, which, being put under the head when going to sleep, doth effectually give true dreams of whatever the mind hath before determined or f consulted upon, the practice of which is as follows:

Thou shalt make an image of the Sun, the figure whereof must be a man sleeping upon the bosom of an angel; which thou shalt make when Leo ascends, the Sun being in the ninth house in Aries; then you must write upon the figure the name of the effect desired, and in the hand of the angel the name and character of the intelligence of the Sun, which is Michael.

Let the same image be made in Virgo ascending—Mercury being fortunate in Aries in the ninth, or Gemini ascending, Mercury being fortunate in the ninth house in Aquarius—and let him be received by Saturn with a fortunate aspect, and let the name of the spirit (which is Raphael) be written upon it. Let the same likewise be made—Libra ascending, Venus being received from Mercury in Gemini in the ninth house—and write upon it the name of the angel of Venus (which is Anael). Again you may make the same image—Aquarius ascending, Saturn fortunately possessing the ninth in his exaltation, which is Libra—and let there be written upon it the name of the angel of Saturn (which is Cassial). The same may be made with Cancer ascending, the Moon being received by Jupiter and Venus in Pisces, and being fortunately placed in the ninth house—and write upon it the spirit of the Moon (which is Gabriel).

There are likewise made rings of dreams of wonderful efficacy, and there are rings of the Sun and Saturn—and the constellation of them is, when the Sun or Saturn ascend in their exaltation in the ninth, and when the Moon is joined to Saturn in the ninth, and in that sign which was the ninth house of the nativity, and write and engrave upon the rings the name of the spirit of the Sun or Saturn; and by these rules you may know how and by what means to constitute more of yourself.

But know this, that such images work nothing (as they are simply images), except they are vivified by spiritual and celestial virtue, and chiefly by the ardent desire and firm intent of the soul of the operator. But who can give a soul to an image, or make a stone, or metal, or clay, or wood, or wax, or paper, to live? Certainly no man whatever; for this arcanum doth not enter into an artist of a stiff neck. He only hath it who transcends the progress of angels, and comes to the very Archtype Himself. The tables of numbers likewise confer to the receiving of oracles, being duly formed under their own constellations.

Therefore, he who is desirous of receiving true oracles by dreams, let him abstain from supper, from drink, and be otherwise well disposed, so his brain will be free from turbulent vapors; let him also have his bed-chamber fair and clean, exorcised and consecrated; then let him perfume the same with some convenient fumigation, and let him anoint his temples with some unguent efficacious hereunto, and put a ring of dreams upon his finger; then let him take one of the images we have spoken of, and place the same under his head; then let him address himself to sleep, meditating upon that thing which he desires to know. So shall he receive a most certain and undoubted oracle by a dream when the Moon goes through the sign of the ninth revolution of his nativity, and when she is in the ninth sign from the sign of perfection.

This is the way whereby we may obtain all sciences and arts whatsoever, whether astrology, occult philosophy, physic, etc., or else suddenly and perfectly with a true illumination of our intellect, although all inferior familiar spirits whatsoever conduce to this effect, and sometimes also evil spirits sensibly inform us, intrinsically and extrinsically.

CHARM TO CURE THE HEADACHE.—If the pain be on the right side of the head, make a comb out of the right horn of a ram; and if the head be combed with it, it will take away the pain. But if the pain be on the left side of the head, then make a comb out of the left horn of a ram, and if the head be combed therewith, it will stop the pain.

CHARM TO HINDER FROM THE BITE OF A MAD DOG.— The tooth of a mad dog which has bitten any human being, tied in leather and hung at the shoulder, will preserve and keep the wearer from being bitten by any mad dog so long as he wears it. It may be worn next to the skin, or concealed in the clothing.

CHARM TO MAKE A TREE BEAR FRUIT.—The seeds of roses, with mustard seed, and the foot of a weasel, tied together in something, and hung among the boughs or branches of a tree which bears but little fruit, will remedy the defect, and render the tree amazingly fruitful.

CHARM AGAINST TROUBLE IN GENERAL.—Repeat reverently, and with sincere faith, the following words, and you shall be protected in the hour of danger: "He shall deliver thee in six troubles, yea, in seven there shall no evil touch thee; in famine he shall redeem thee from death, and in war from the power of the sword; and thou shalt know that thy tabernacle shall be in peace, and thou shalt visit thy habitation and shall not err."

PALMISTRY.

—

—

I shall now say something of palmistry, which is a judgment of the conditions, inclinations, and fortunes of men and women, from the various lines and characters which nature has imprinted in the hand, which are almost as various as the hands that have them. And to render what I shall say more plain. I will, in the first place, present the scheme or figures of the hand, and explain the various lines therein:

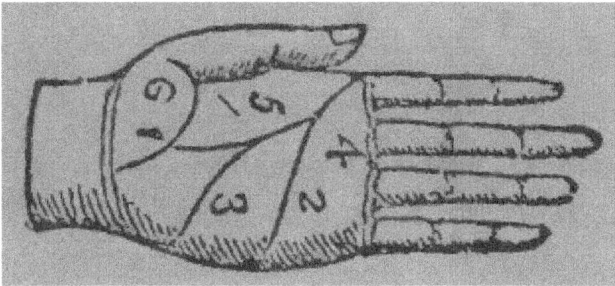

1. *Line of Life.*
2. *Table Line.*
3. *Natural Line.*
4. *Girdle of Venus.*
5. *Line of Death.*
6. *Mount of Venus.*

By this figure the reader will see that one of these lines, and which, indeed, is reckoned the principal, is called the line of life; this line encloses the thumb, separating it from the hollow of the hand. The next to it, which is called the natural line, takes its beginning from the rising of the forefinger, near the line of life, and reaches to the table line, and generally makes a triangle. The table line, commonly called the line of fortune, begins under the little linger, and ends near the middle finger. The girdle of Venus, which is another line so called, begins near the joint of the little finger, and ends between the forefinger and the middle linger The line of death is that which plainly appears in a counter line to that of life, and is by some called the sister line, ending usually at the other end; for when the line of life is ending, death Comes, and it can go no further. There are also lines in fleshy parts, as in the ball of the thumb, which is called the mount of Venus, under each of the fingers, are called mounts, which are each one governed by a several planet; and the hollow of the hand is called the plain of Mars.

I now proceed to give judgment of these several lines. And, in the first place, take notice that in palmistry the left hand is chiefly to be regarded; because therein the lines are most visible, and have the strictest communication with the heart and brains. Now, having premised these, in the next place observe the line of life, and if it be fair, extended to its full length, and not broken with an intermixture of cross lines, it shows long life and health; and it is the same if a double line of life appears, as there sometimes does. When the stars appear in this line it is a significator of great losses and calamities; if on it there appear the figure of two O's, or a Y, it threatens the person with blindness. If it wraps itself about the table line, then does it promise wealth and honor to be attained by prudence and industry; if the line be cut or jagged at the upper end. it denotes much sickness. If this line be cut by any line coming from the mount of Venus, it declares the person to be unfortunate in love, and business also, and threatens him with sudden death.

A cross between the line of life and the table line shows the person to be very liberal and charitable, and of a noble spirit. Let us now see the signification of the table line.

The table line, when broad, and of a lovely color, shows a healthful constitution and a quiet and contented mind and courageous spirit. But if it has crosses towards the little finger, it threatens the party with much affliction by sickness. If the line be doubled, or divided in three parts, in any of the extremities, it shows the party to be of a generous temper, and of a good fortune to support it; but if this line be forked at the end, it threatens the person shall suffer by jealousies, fears, and doubts, and with the loss of riches got by deceit. If three points such as these... are found in it, they denote the person prudent and liberal, a lover of learning and of good temper. If it spreads itself to the fore and middle fingers, and ends blunt, it denotes preferment. Let us now see what is signified by the middle finger:

The line has in it sometimes (for there is scarce one hand in which it varies not) divers significant characters. Many small lines between this and the table line threatens the party with sickness, and also gives him hopes of recovery. A half cross branching into this line declares the person shall have honor, riches, and good success in all his undertakings. A half moon denotes cold and watery distempers, but a sun or star upon this line promiseth prosperity and riches. This line doubled in a woman shows she will have several husbands, but without any children by them.

The line of Venus, if it happens to be cut or divided near the forefinger, threatens ruin to the party, and that it shall befall him by means of a lascivious woman and bad company. Two crosses upon this line, one being on the forefinger, and the other bending towards the little finger, shows the party to be weak and inclined to modesty and virtue; and, indeed, it generally denotes modesty in women; and, therefore, those who desire such wives usually choose them by this standard.

The liver line, if it be straight and crossed by other lines, shows the person to be of a sound judgment and a piercing understanding; but if it be winding, crooked, and bending outward, it shows deceit and flattery, and that the person is not to be trusted. If it makes a triangle, or a quadrangle, it shows a person to be of a noble descent and ambitious.

The plain of Mars being in the hollow of the hand, or if the line passes through it, which renders it very plain, is fortunate; this plain being hollowed, and the lines crooked and distorted, threaten the party to fall by his ill-conduct. When the lines begin at the wrist, long within the plain, reaching the brown of the hand, they show the person to be one given to quarrelling, often in broils, and of a hot and fiery spirit, by which he shall suffer much damage. If deep, large crosses in the middle of the plain, it shows the party shall obtain honor by martial exploits; but if it be a woman, that she shall have several husbands, and easy labor with her children.

The line of death is fatal when any crosses or broken lines appear in it; for they threaten the person with sickness and short life. A clouded moon appearing there, threatens a child-bed woman with death. A bloody spot in the line denotes a violent death. A star like a comet threatens ruin by war and death by pestilence; but if a bright sun appear therein, it promises long life and prosperity.

As for the lines in the wrist, being fair, they denote good fortune, but if crossed and broken, the contrary.

Thus much with respect to the several lines in the hand. Now as to the judgment to be made from the hand itself; if the hand be soft and long, and lean withal, it denotes a person of a good understanding, a lover of peace, and honest, discreet, serviceable, a good neighbor, and a lover of learning. He whose hands are very thick and very short, is thereby signified to be faithful, strong, and laborious, and one that cannot long retain his anger. He whose hands are full of hairs, and those hairs thick and great ones, and his finger withal be crooked, he is thereby noted to be luxurious, vain, false, of a dull understanding, and disposition, and more foolish than wise. He whose hands and fingers do bend upwards is commonly a man liberal, serviceable, a keeper of secrecy, and apt to be poor (for he is seldom fortunate), to do any man courtesy. He whose hand is stiff and will not bend at the upper joint, near his finger, is always a wretched, miserable person, covetous, obstinate, incredulous, and one that will believe nothing that contradicts his own private interest. And thus much shall suffice to be said of judgment made by palmistry.

Finger-Nail Observations.

—

Broad nails show the person to be bashful, fearful, but of gentle nature. When there is a certain white mark at the extremity of them, it shows that the person has more honesty than subtlety, and that his worldly substance will be impaired through negligence. White nails and long denote much sickness and infirmity, especially fevers, an indication of strength and deceit by women. If upon the white anything appears at the extremity that is pale, it denotes short life by sudden death, and the person to be given to melancholy. When there appears a certain mixed redness, of divers colors, at the beginning of the nails, it shows the person to be choleric and quarrelsome. When the extremity is black it is a sign of husbandry. Narrow nails denote the person to be inclined to mischief, and to do injury to his neighbor. Long nails show the person to be good-natured, but mistrustful, and loves reconciliation rather than differences. Oblique nails signify deceit and want of courage. Little and round nails denote obstinate anger and hatred. If they be crooked at the extremity, they show pride and fierceness. Round nails show a choleric person, yet soon reconciled, honest, and a lover of secret sciences. Fleshy nails denote the person to be mild in his temper, idle, and lazy. Pale and black nails show the person to be very deceitful to his neighbor, and subject to many diseases. Red and marked nails signify a choleric and martial nature, given to cruelty; and, as many little marks as there are, they speak of so many evil desires.

SEVERAL CHARACTERS OR SEMBLANCES OF LETTERS, AND LINES IN THE HAND, AS THEY TEND TO SIGNIFY MANY THINGS, ACCORDING TO THE ART OF PALMISTRY, ETC.

———

There are in this case divers letters, lines appearing in the hand, by which the wise in all ages have given judgment in the foregoing premises.

If the letter A be found on the Mount of Jupiter, or at the root of the middle finger, promises growing fortune, and, perhaps, considerable preferments by the favor of princes and great men.

If B be found on the Mount of the Sun, which is at the root of the finger, it signifies length of days, prosperity and much to be beloved, as also a virtuous person.

If C, with a star over, appears on the Mount of Venus, it gives the person early and happy life.

If the letter L be on the Mount of Saturn, which is at the root of the middle finger, and cut with cross lines, it denotes the party to be under much affliction, to be given to melancholy, and short-lived.

The letter K on the Mount of Mercury, which is at the root of the little finger, denotes the party to rise to preferment by ingenuity and marriage.

The letter D on the Mount of the Moon denotes the party kind, good-natured, and much beloved.

The letter G in the Plain of Mars, near the Line of Life, speaks the party to be of a violent temper, given to anger, and threatens him or her with sudden untimely death; however, to a woman it promises a husband that grows great in military affairs; and thus much for characters of this kind.

DIVINATION.

—

How to obtain some Knowledge of Future Events.

—

Any person fasting on midsummer eve, and sitting in the church porch, will, at midnight, see the spirits of the persons of that parish, who will die that year, come and knock at the church-door in the order and succession in which they will die. One of these watchers, there being several in company, fell into a profound sleep, so that he could not be waked; whilst in this state his ghost was seen by the rest of his companions knocking at the church-door. Any unmarried woman fasting on midsummer eve, and at midnight laying a clean cloth, with bread, cheese, and ale, and sitting down as if going to eat, the street-door being left open, the person whom she is afterward to marry will come into the room, and drink to her by bowing; and afterward filling the glass, will leave it on the table, and making another bow, retire. On St. Agnes's night, the 21st of January, take a row of pins, and pull out every one, one after another, saying a paternoster, on sticking a pin in your sleeve, and you will dream of him you shall marry. Another method to see a future spouse in a dream: the party inquiring must lie in a different country from that in which he commonly resides, and, on going to bed, must knit the left garter about the right-legged stocking, letting the other garter and stocking alone; and as you rehearse the following verses, at every comma knit a knot:

This knot I knit,
To know a thing I know not yet,
That I may see
The man that shall my husband be,
How he goes and what he wears,
And what he does all days and years.

Accordingly, in a dream he will appear with the insignia of his trade or profession. Another performed by charming the moon, thus: At the first appearance of the new moon, immediately after the new year's day, go out in the evening and stand over the spears of a gate or stile, and, looking on the moon, repeat the following lines:

All hail to thee, moon! all hail to thee,
I prithee, good moon, reveal to me
This night who my husband must be.

The party will then dream of their future husband. A slice of the bride-cake, thrice thrown through the wedding-ring, and laid under the head of an unmarried woman, will make them dream of their future husband. The same is practiced in the North with a piece of the groaning cheese.

TRADITIONAL WAY TO

—

Baffle Your Enemies.

—

Repeat reverently, and with sincere faith, the following words, and you will be protected in the hour of danger:

"Behold, God is my salvation; I will trust, and not be afraid, for the Lord Jehovah is my strength and my song; he also is become my salvation.

"For the stars of heaven, and the constellation thereof, shall not give their light; the sun shall he darkened in his going forth, and the moon shall not cause her light to shine.

"And behold, at, eventide, trouble; and before morning he is not; this is the portion of them that spoil us, and the lot of them that rob us."

Made in the USA
Las Vegas, NV
03 December 2020